AN OXFAM REPORT ON INTERNATIONAL RESPONSIBILITY FOR POVERTY IN NAMIBIA

First Published 1986
© Oxfam 1986

ISBN 0 85598 076 1

Printed in Great Britain by Express Litho Service (Oxford)

Published by Oxfam
274 Banbury Road
Oxford OX2 7DZ
United Kingdom

Acknowledgements

My main thanks must go to all the Namibian people who generously gave their time and expertise to help with the research for this book, particularly Oxfam friends and partners.

I am also grateful to the Overseas Development Administration, the Foreign & Commonwealth Office, the Catholic Institute for International Relations and the Namibian Support Committee for their assistance in providing information.

Thanks are especially due for the time and advice given by all those who read and commented on the drafts. In particular, I am grateful to Richard Moorsom who helped with both research and editing, and to Justin Ellis, Julio Faundez, Peter Katjavivi, Prudence Smith, Paul Spray and Brian Wood.

This book reflects the collective experience of Oxfam's work in Namibia over the past twenty-two years and I have therefore relied on the active collaboration of Oxfam staff and trustees. Sue Coxhead deserves special thanks for her help with research and typing.

Finally, without the special help with childcare given by Mandy Bristow, Caroline Lovick and Prudence Smith, the book would never have seen the light of day.

Susanna Smith
March 1986

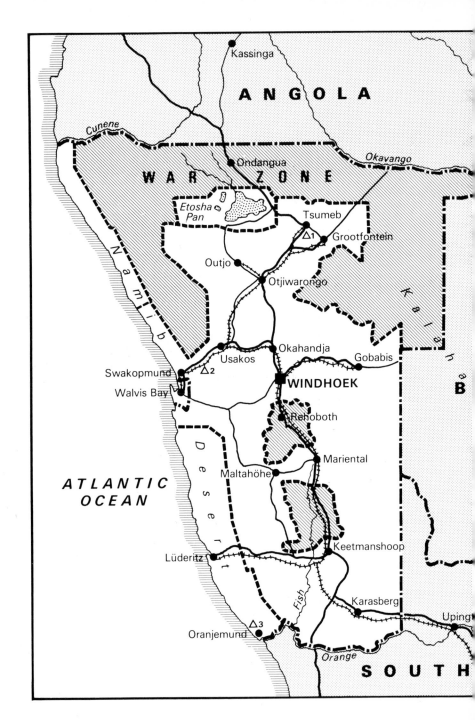

ZAMBIA

Zambezi

rivi Strip

Okavango
Swamp

SWANA

sert

AFRICA

Zaire

Tanzania

Angola   Zambia

Zimbabwe

NAMIBIA   Botswana   Mozambique

Swaziland

South
Africa   Lesotho

Map 1: Namibia and its neighbours

Map 2: Namibia

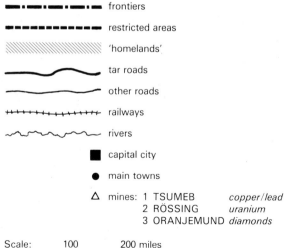

▬▪▬▪▬▪▬▪▬   frontiers

▬▬▬▬▬▬▬   restricted areas

▨▨▨▨▨▨   'homelands'

⌇⌇⌇⌇   tar roads

⌇⌇⌇⌇   other roads

┼┼┼┼┼┼┼┼   railways

～～～～   rivers

■   capital city

●   main towns

△   mines: 1 TSUMEB   *copper/lead*
               2 RÖSSING   *uranium*
               3 ORANJEMUND *diamonds*

Scale: 100   200 miles

Adapted from *The Namibians*, the Minority Rights Group
report no. 19, London, 1985.

Contents

NAMIBIA
Basic Facts

Government International law recognises the United Nations Council for Namibia as the legal administering authority for Namibia, and in turn the United Nations recognises the South West Africa People's Organisation (SWAPO) as the *"sole authentic representative"* of the people. However, Namibia is illegally occupied by South Africa. Namibia is referred to by South Africa as 'South West Africa/Namibia'.

Capital Windhoek.

Area 824,000 km^2 — over 3 times the size of the UK, and 2/3 the size of South Africa.

Population (1983)[1] 1.46 million. Black 94%, white 6%. 70% of the black population is rural. Approximate growth rate of black population 3%.

Language Oshivambo is the main indigenous language group, and is spoken by half the black population. Afrikaans is the main official language.

Land Ownership 5,000 large white-owned farms occupy 77% of all the viable farming land. 190,000 black peasant farming households are crowded onto fragments of inferior land and desert on the fringe of the white-owned farming land.[2]

Economy (1983)[3] GDP per capita R1,400 ($1,259)
GNP per capita R1,200 ($1,079)
GNP is normally 25-30% below GDP. The difference is wealth made in Namibia but sent abroad, mostly as corporate profits.
Main exports: diamonds, uranium oxide, base metals, beef/cattle, karakul (lamb pelts used for fur coats), fish and fish products.

Distribution of wealth (1983)[4]	GDP per capita	— whites	R5,800	($5,168)
		— blacks	R330	($297)
		— black peasants	R130	($117)

Health Infant Mortality Rate (per 1,000 live births)[5]
— for blacks 155
— for whites 21

Education — 60% of black adults are illiterate.[6]
— Only 1% of black adults have completed secondary education.[7]
— Schooling is compulsory for white children, but not for black.
— Per capita, the state spends over five times more on white children's education than on black children's.[8]

Chronology

1820 – 30s   Orlams and other Khoisan groups move north from Cape Province.

1850   Jonker Afrikander (Nama leader) defeats Hereros.

1862 – 70   Nama-Herero Wars.

1868   British Commissioner sent from Cape Town.

1876   Boers trek to north-east of territory.

1878   Walvis Bay (today Namibia's only deep-water port) annexed by Britain.

1884 – 85   **German colonial period starts** following Berlin Conference. German expropriation of Namibian land begins. Walvis Bay taken over by the Cape Colony, now part of South Africa.

1888   Maharero, Herero chief, forces Germans to withdraw from his capital.

1889   First German troops arrive.

1890   Germany annexes territory.

1892   German troops massacre Namas.

1894   Another defeat of the Namas; Herero rebellion crushed.

1904   Ovambos defeat Portuguese expedition at Naulila.

1904 – 07   Namas and Hereros revolt again. German colonial administration adopts genocide policy against Herero people; over 80,000 Namibians killed. Cattle and land confiscated for settler farmers.

1908   Discovery of diamonds leads to mineral rush and growth of settlement.

1914   Outbreak of World War I; South Africa aligns with Britain against Germany.

1915   **South African colonial period starts**

Germany surrenders Namibia to South African troops.

Military administration of Namibia by South Africa.

1919	Treaty of Versailles at end of World War I. Germany's colonies confiscated and redistributed.
1920	Namibia placed under League of Nations mandate to be administered by South Africa on behalf of the British Crown.
1922	South Africa establishes 'reserves' and starts to distribute land to settlers.
1925	Legislative Council established — with all-white electorate.
1939	Outbreak of World War II; South Africa sends troops to Namibia to prevent pro-Hitler coup by German settlers. Many Namibian and South African blacks serve in the South African forces, fighting against Nazi Germany.
1946	South Africa refuses to hand over mandate for Namibia to United Nations (UN) trusteeship on grounds that it does not recognise UN as successor to League of Nations.
1948	Victory of Afrikaner National Party in South Africa; beginning of modern apartheid legislation.
1949	First petition by Namibians to UN for end of South African rule.
1950	International Court of Justice unanimous decision that mandate is still in existence (contrary to South African claim that it ceased with the League of Nations).

Protest against 'removals' in Windhoek, twelve killed, fifty wounded when police open fire. |
1957	Ovamboland People's Congress founded, the precursor to SWAPO (South West Africa People's Organisation), Namibia's national liberation movement.
1960	SWAPO founded.
1961	Ethiopia and Liberia apply to the International Court of Justice (ICJ) to end South Africa's League of Nations mandate.
1964	Odendaal Commission's report outlines a blueprint for the establishment of separate 'homelands' for Namibia's black people.
1965	Organisation of African Unity recognises SWAPO as the liberation movement of Namibia.
1966	The UN General Assembly revokes South Africa's mandate over Namibia, and orders South Africa to withdraw. South Africa refuses. SWAPO starts military offensive, marking beginning of liberation war against South Africa's forces.
1967	United Nations Council for Namibia (UNCN) established to administer Namibia on the UN's behalf until independence. The UNCN has been denied access to Namibia, by South Africa, ever since.

1968	South Africa begins to implement 'homelands' policy in Namibia. Thirty-eight SWAPO members, including Ja Toivo (currently SWAPO Secretary General), put on trial in Pretoria on terrorism charges: twenty-one sentenced to life imprisonment on Robben Island.
1971	The ICJ gives its Advisory Opinion that South Africa occupies Namibia illegally.
1973	SWAPO recognised by the UN as the *"sole authentic representative"* of the Namibian people.
1974	The UNCN passes its **Decree no. 1 for the Protection of Namibia's Natural Resources** requiring UNCN consent for any exploitation of natural resources undertaken by foreign companies.
1975	Angola becomes independent and gives SWAPO new military bases. South Africa starts the Turnhalle Constitutional Conference in an attempt to promote client political groupings inside Namibia and thus bypass SWAPO's political influence.
1977	South Africa appoints an Administrator-General for Namibia with full legislative and executive powers. South Africa re-annexes Walvis Bay.
	The UK, USA, Canada, France and West Germany form the Contact Group to negotiate with South Africa over Namibia's independence.
1978	Contact Group's proposals incorporated in UN Security Council (SC) Resolution 435 for free and fair elections aimed at leading to early independence. Resolution accepted both by SWAPO and South Africa. But South Africa has rejected the UN programme for implementation ever since.
	Contrary to the terms of SC Resolution 435, South Africa holds internal elections (boycotted by SWAPO) and then installs the Democratic Turnhalle Alliance (DTA) of client political groups as the National Assembly with wide legislative powers. International community refuses to acknowledge the new interim government which is declared **null and void** by the UN Security Council.
	South African commando raid kills 700 Namibian refugees in Angola. War intensifies.
1980	Compulsory military service in the South African armed forces extended to black Namibians.
	South Africa mounts further military incursions into Angola.
1981	UN Pre-Implementation Meeting, Geneva. South Africa says it is premature to proceed towards ceasefire.
	New US administration, under President Reagan, introduces 'linkage' policy making Namibia's independence conditional on the withdrawal of Cuban troops stationed in Angola.

More South African military attacks in Angola.

Southern African 'frontline' states call for economic sanctions against South Africa to pressurise it to accept implementation of SC Resolution 435.

1983 DTA administration collapses and the South African-appointed Administrator-General assumes direct rule.

France leaves Contact Group in protest at US 'linkage' policy.

South Africa invades Angola again.

1984 SWAPO and South African officials meet in Zambia and Cape Verde. No agreement due to South Africa's insistence on 'linkage' and South Africa's refusal to abide by terms of Resolution 435.

UN Secretary blames 'linkage' issue for stalemate, saying that agreement had been reached on all other outstanding issues.

Military conscription of Namibian blacks extends age limit to 55.

1985 'Multi-Party Conference' (MPC) administration unilaterally announced as 'interim government' by South Africa to replace failed DTA. MPC is boycotted by SWAPO and condemned by Churches in Namibia, the Non-Aligned Movement, the EEC and unilaterally by western nations including Britain.

Mass arrests by police and army in Namibia as civilians demonstrate against the new 'interim government'.

South African troops mount largest-ever military exercise in Namibia called **Vuiswys**, Afrikaans for 'fist-showing'.

The Commonwealth Nassau Communiqué in October condemns South Africa's continued illegal occupation, and agrees on limited sanctions against South Africa on these grounds, **inter alia**.

1986 South African President, P.W. Botha, announces implementation of SC Resolution 435 from August 1, provided agreement is reached on withdrawal of Cuban troops from Angola. South Africa's continued insistence on 'linkage' remains unacceptable to SWAPO, the Angolan Government and UN. The stalemate over Namibia's independence continues.

Introduction

Namibia is one of the wealthiest countries in Africa, with rich mineral deposits, fertile coastal fishing grounds and plenty of good stock-farming land. Yet the majority of Namibians live in extreme poverty. The facts in this report show emphatically that their poverty is directly caused by the economic, political and social policies and structures imposed on Namibia by South Africa.

Successive land expropriation first by the German and then by the South African colonial authorities has robbed Namibians of their economic independence. Forced into reserves on land which the white settlers did not want, black Namibians have been systematically pauperised. However, it is **their** labour which has built the prosperity of the colonial economy.

Women, unemployed men, children and the old are imprisoned by poverty in urban slums and in the 'homelands' where they must scratch a living as best they can. Whereas the South African-controlled administration ensures good health care and education for the whites, services for the black majority are grossly inadequate. In contrast to the opulent lifestyle enjoyed by the white minority, the poverty endured by the majority seems all the more appalling. This inequality means that a black baby is over seven times more likely to die in infancy than a white baby.[1]

Impoverished and oppressed by apartheid rule, the Namibian people are also suffering the devastating effects of military occupation. An estimated 100,000 members of the South African Defence Force presently occupy Namibia as a result of the bitter war being waged in the north with SWAPO guerillas.[2] This makes Namibia one of the most intensively occupied countries in the world.[3] Some 75-80,000 Namibians have left their country, fleeing from poverty, oppression and military occupation.[4]

Oxfam has been funding small-scale development and humanitarian projects in Namibia since 1964 and providing humanitarian assistance to Namibian refugees. Based on this experience, Oxfam's view is that the widespread poverty and underdevelopment which exists today is preventable. However, only after independence will Namibia's people have the power to begin to reshape their society and transform the inequitable structures which cause and perpetuate their poverty.

After independence huge problems will of course remain. In writing this book Oxfam's aim is to raise awareness of the suffering of the Namibian people and to create a sense of urgency over the need for independence. The interminable high-level UN negotiations over Namibia's independence have made the issue seem remote and confusing. The basic problem is, however, very simple: two decades since the UN General Assembly ordered South Africa to withdraw, Namibia remains the last country in Africa under white colonial rule.

In 1920 South Africa took over the administration of Namibia on behalf of the British Crown, under a League of Nations mandate. Under its terms South Africa was mandated to *"promote to the utmost the material and moral well-being and the social progress of the inhabitants of the territory"*.[5] However, in spite of its acceptance of this mandate and of *"a sacred trust for civilisation"* for Namibia's people,[6] successive South African governments have imposed apartheid policies on Namibia and drained the country of its riches.

The UN, in 1945, took over trusteeship of territories previously under League of Nations mandates. South Africa refused to give up its mandate, demanding the right to annex Namibia. This was rejected by the UN General Assembly and the long and fruitless international deliberations over Namibia began.

In 1971 the International Court of Justice declared that South Africa's occupation of Namibia was illegal. But Namibia remains an international pawn, its future tied up with superpower politics and foreign economic interests. The five western countries with the biggest economic stake in Namibia — Britain, West Germany, the United States, France and Canada — set themselves up in 1977 as the 'Contact Group' to negotiate with South Africa the terms of Namibia's independence. These negotiations led to the UN Security Council's Resolution 435, outlining the terms for free and fair elections and full independence. Resolution 435 is the most important internationally acceptable statement of intent, which has governed all diplomacy concerning Namibia since its adoption in 1978.

Although the South African Government agreed to the terms of Resolution 435, it has prevaricated ever since over the UN implementation programme.

South Africa's evasion of UN control on this issue lies at the heart of the political deadlock over Namibia's independence. Other states with substantial economic interests in South Africa have lacked sufficient political will to enforce implementation of Resolution 435.

The deadlock was compounded in 1981 when the new US administration introduced the concept of 'linkage' into the negotiations, insisting that Namibia's independence should be conditional on the withdrawal of Cuban troops from Angola. (The Cuban troops had been invited into newly-independent Angola in November 1975 to repel attacks by UNITA forces and the South African military.[7])

Although the UN and the other Contact Group states declared that 'linkage' was irrelevant to implementation of Resolution 435, the United States has continued to promote it as a key condition of Namibian independence.

France resigned from the Contact Group in protest at the introduction of 'linkage', but Britain has taken a different view. After his visit to some of the southern African 'frontline' states in January 1985, the UK

Oxfam's Namibia Programme

Oxfam has been funding small-scale development and humanitarian projects in Namibia since 1964, and has been providing humanitarian assistance to Namibian refugees.[1]

Inside Namibia, Oxfam has supported a range of projects. One example is a small scheme in the south of the country where local people have organised their own independent school . As well as providing a decent education, the school also runs its own garden where the parents grow fruit and vegetables for the children and for the old people in the area. In this way, the most vulnerable sections of their community have an improved diet, and there is a little left over for sale to raise funds for the school. Fresh garden produce is otherwise hard to come by. In the shops, fruit and vegetables are expensive and usually far from fresh as they are generally imported by road from South Africa.

Another example is a community crèche in Katatura, the township reserved for 'blacks' outside Windhoek. Many poor women, particularly those who are bringing up families alone, find daytime childcare for the under-sevens a problem as there are no state nurseries to care for children while their mothers are out at work or looking for work. As a result, pre-school children are often left all day to fend for themselves in the streets. The crèche provides a secure, daytime home for fifteen such children. As one of the crèche workers explained:

"Our aim is to help some of the poor women of Katatura. We are all so poor that we have to rely on each other if we are to survive. Our crèche has been running for one year now, and you can see how well the children are getting on. Their mothers are so happy to have the crèche, because now they don't have the terrible anxiety of leaving their children alone while they go to work." [2]

A third example is the literacy training undertaken by the Namibian Literacy Programme (NLP), a voluntary organisation which organises adult learners' groups throughout the country. One NLP worker explained:

"We are working to help people overcome the enormous educational inequalities in this country. Illiteracy is a big social handicap, and the majority of adults are illiterate. People join our groups for all sorts of reasons. For example, a lot of women join so that they will be able to write letters to their husbands working away from home as migrant labourers." [3]

Secretary of State for Foreign and Commonwealth Affairs, Sir Geoffrey Howe, stated: *"One must recognise that the best possible prospect for settlement lies in the negotiations now led by the United States. Linkage was no part of the Security Council's Resolution. We do not recognise it as a precondition for settlement, but the fact that a linkage has been made cannot be ignored if a settlement is to be reached."* [8]

During 1985, international opinion against South Africa hardened, largely due to the South African Government's violent reaction to growing black civilian resistance to apartheid. This provoked renewed international concern and many western nations decided to impose

Oxfam Grants To Namibian Projects For The Last Four Financial Years

1982 – 83	£ 3,918
1983 – 84	62,511
1984 – 85	84,609
1985 – 86 (to 30.3.86)	84,037

Children playing at an Oxfam-funded community crèche in Katatura.

Suzanne Williams

limited economic sanctions against South Africa to increase the pressure for change.

However, notwithstanding this increased international focus on South Africa, the stalemate over negotiations for a just settlement in Namibia continues. The once-active Contact Group has faded into inaction and Britain appears to be passively backing American diplomatic initiatives. Despite President P W Botha's recently announced deadline of August 1st 1986 for beginning implementation of Resolution 435, the condition of 'linkage' to the withdrawal of Cuban troops from Angola remains a major stumbling block.

The prospect of Namibia attaining an internationally recognised independence is still bleak. However, if the international community were to join together and press unconditionally for Namibia's long-denied right to independence, South Africa would find it hard to sustain its illegal occupation.

The challenge facing Britain is clear. There is now an urgent need to consider new measures to secure Namibia's unconditional independence, to relieve the poverty, distress and suffering of the Namibian people.

Heather Hughson

Summary of the main terms of United Nations Security Council Resolution 435 [3]

- Free and fair elections for the whole of Namibia as one political entity, under the supervision and control of the UN.
- Universal adult suffrage.
- Elections to be held for a Constituent Assembly which will adopt a Constitution for an independent Namibia. The Constitution to determine the organisation and powers of all levels of government.
- Before the start of the electoral campaign, the Administrator-General of Namibia to repeal all remaining discriminatory or restrictive laws, regulations, or administrative measures which might prejudice that objective.
- Before the start of the electoral campaign, the release of all Namibian political prisoners or political detainees held by the South African authorities should be arranged so that they may participate freely in the electoral process.
- All Namibian refugees to be permitted to return peacefully and participate fully in the electoral process, and the UN to ensure that Namibians in exile are given a free and voluntary choice whether to return.
- A binding ceasefire by all parties and the restriction of South African and SWAPO armed forces to base. Thereafter a phased withdrawal from Namibia of the majority of South African troops.
- All unilateral measures taken by the illegal government in Namibia in relation to the electoral process, including unilateral registration of voters or transfer of power, are null and void.

CHAPTER 1

THE ECONOMY:
Wealth based on poverty

Namibia is one of the wealthiest countries in Africa, with a per capita GDP in 1983 of R1,400 ($1,259),[1] but the wealth is very unevenly distributed. In Oxfam's experience some of the worst examples of chronic poverty and suffering in Africa are to be found amongst Namibia's black population, alongside the wealthy and privileged lifestyle enjoyed by the minority white population. The average ratio of white to black incomes is about 18:1,[2] though recent moves by South Africa to promote a black elite of salaried civil servants and political appointees has reduced this discrepancy for some blacks.

The basis of the country's wealth is its abundant natural resources: land, minerals, the sea and, above all, the people, who have been robbed of their economic independence and kept grindingly poor. The basis of the people's poverty is the unchecked exploitation and export of the country's wealth by South African, British and other foreign interests.

Poverty for the majority is created in two main ways. Firstly, much of Namibia's wealth is exported by foreign investors.[3] Secondly, the colonial structure of the economy means that wealth remaining inside the country is almost entirely in white hands. Even the taxes raised by the government are disproportionately spent on services for whites. Moreover, foreign companies employ whites in nearly all the best-paid and supervisory jobs. In 1983, only about 22% of GDP was left over for the black population, who formed 94.5% of the total population. Of this 22% of GDP, about two thirds went on wages to workers, another tenth represented the earnings of small business people and traders, leaving only a quarter for the peasant population.[4] Thus, barely 6% of GDP was left over for the peasant population, by far the largest section of black society.

The sheer profitability of colonialism has meant that Namibia's Gross National Product (retained in country) has been consistently lower, by 25-30%, than its Gross Domestic Product (produced in country). The difference is wealth created in Namibia but sent abroad, mostly as corporate profits. The severe recession reduced the difference in 1983 to about 15%.[5]

PEOPLE

Namibia's people have been endlessly exploited in the interests of the prosperous colonial economy. The comprehensive nature of colonial social engineering has affected every important aspect of daily life for blacks. As one black worker explained:

"Politics affects everything we do. For example, we can't expect equal pay for equal work, so we can't ever be in a position to choose freely where we live, as the white areas in town are too expensive for us." [6]

Distribution of Namibia's GDP (1983)

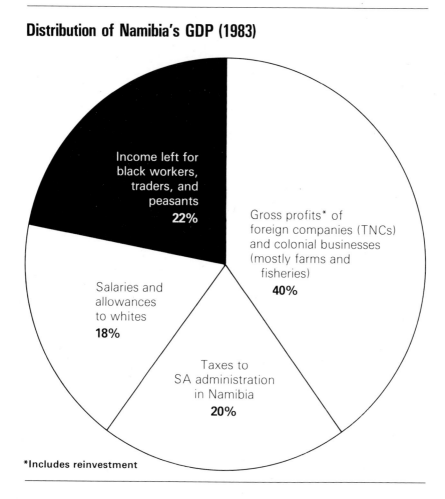

Income left for black workers, traders, and peasants
22%

Gross profits* of foreign companies (TNCs) and colonial businesses (mostly farms and fisheries)
40%

Salaries and allowances to whites
18%

Taxes to SA administration in Namibia
20%

*Includes reinvestment

Map 3: Settlement patterns before colonisation

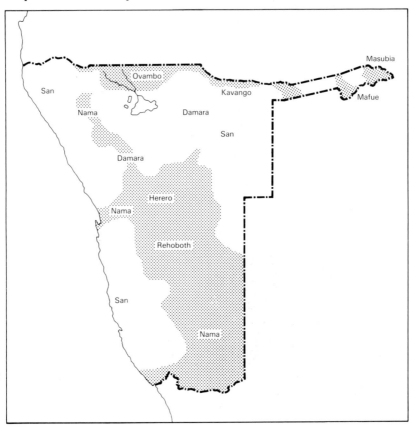

Main areas of settlement

Source: R.H. Green, M. & K. Kiljunen, *Namibia: the Last Colony*, Longman, Harlow, 1981.

The 'Homelands'

The principal way in which the South African authorities have controlled Namibia's black population is by dividing them up into 'ethnic groups', and by instituting a 'homelands' policy corresponding to the apartheid concept of 'ethnicity'. The 'homelands' policy consolidated previous land appropriation, whereby blacks were forced off their land into labour reserves.

The present-day 'homelands' policy began with the South African Government's appointment of the Odendaal Commission which was set

Map 4: 'Homelands' according to the Odendaal plan

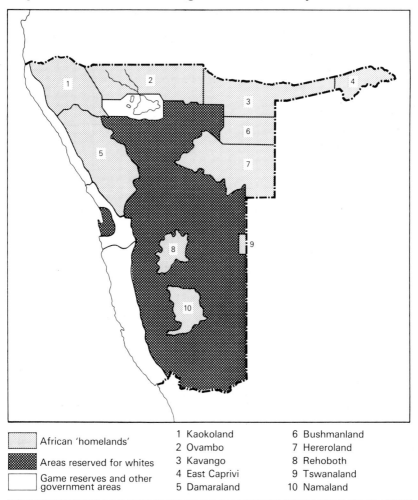

░	African 'homelands'	1 Kaokoland	6 Bushmanland
		2 Ovambo	7 Hereroland
▓	Areas reserved for whites	3 Kavango	8 Rehoboth
	Game reserves and other	4 East Caprivi	9 Tswanaland
☐	government areas	5 Damaraland	10 Namaland

up in 1962 to devise an apartheid blueprint for Namibia. In 1964, the Commission's report was completed. It proposed to divide the Namibian people up into twelve 'population groups', each with its own 'homeland' and associated constitutional trappings but none of the powers of independent government. Thus the aim was to prevent blacks, as a unified political force, from participating in national government by sealing them off into small, internal, quasi-nation states outside which they would have no political rights, and inside which their political rights would be restricted.

Implementation of the Commission's plan was held back pending international developments, but by 1968 South Africa judged that it could go ahead.[7] New laws in 1968 and 1969 set the framework for constructing the 'homelands' edifice.[8] **The Development of Self-Government for Native Nations in South West Africa Act (1968)** provided for the creation, for each 'homeland', of a legislative council with nominal ordinance-making powers and an executive council with corresponding administrative powers. However, important matters such as control of the military, police, foreign affairs and the amendment or repeal of the Act itself were excluded.[9]

Extensive amendments to the 1968 Act were made by an act passed in 1973 which enabled the 'homelands' to become 'self-governing' as a transitional phase prior to South Africa's conception of 'independence'.[10] The 1973 Act allowed for each self-governing area to have a cabinet consisting of a chief minister and other ministers.

After further delays caused by the transformation of the Turnhalle Constitutional Conference into a National Assembly, the Administrator-General for Namibia (appointed in 1977 by the South African Government as the colonial governor) introduced Proclamation AG8 in 1980. This provided for a second tier of government (underneath the then DTA-dominated central administration), for each of Namibia's officially classified 'ethnic groups'. The introduction of these second-tier governments, also called 'representative authorities', or 'ethnic administrations', was partly intended to make the 'homelands' policy more palatable to international opinion. The geographical emphasis of the previous 'homelands' legal arrangements was dropped in favour of a definition which characterised each 'representative authority' as responsible for the governmental matters of each 'population group', wherever resident. But this is widely held to be a merely cosmetic distinction since the administration centre for each 'population group' remains in the previously proclaimed 'homeland' area. In any case the very existence of separate governmental structures for each racial group, and for each 'population group' amongst blacks, however presented, is clearly a mechanism to promote 'divide and rule'.

Each 'representative authority' consists of a legislative assembly and executive committee with local control over such matters as education, health, housing, social welfare, agriculture, taxes, land tenure, civil defence and internal security. But vital matters of national importance such as foreign affairs, international negotiations, overall national planning, and command over the military remain in the hands of the South African-controlled central administration, under the Administrator-General who has authority to veto any decisions it takes.[11]

Twelve 'population groups' were originally classified by the Odendaal Commission, and ten 'homelands' for blacks were officially designated during the main implementation phase from 1968 to 1977.[12] Three of these have been given 'self-governing' status, and the others various forms of tribal authority such as advisory boards or councils.

In practice, black Namibians are not divided in the way which the apartheid classification suggests. Many are of mixed descent from different 'ethnic groups'. Some groups are closely related to each other, many live closely together, and urbanisation tends to break down rural divisions. The Namibian Churches act as a cohesive force, and the national liberation movement, led by SWAPO, has tried to create a national identity in its attempt to overcome the imposed divisions.

Susanna Smith

"I am a Namibian. I have lived and worked in every part of this country. My children and grandchildren are also Namibians."

25

Repressive Legislation

Since the beginning of the colonial era, a wide range of laws has been introduced to control and exploit the black labour force. Together with the poverty created by land appropriation, these laws have ensured a continuous supply of cheap labour. They have served both to restrict black people's movement and their residency rights. Other punitive laws appear designed to keep blacks in a servile position and prevent the growing impact of the national liberation movement.

In order to serve the labour requirements of the colonial economy, two forms of discrimination against blacks were used, related to job sector and to supposed place of residence. The aim was to prevent a free labour market and thus to keep down labour costs : Accordingly, each commercial sector was allocated its own reservoir of cheap black labour and various 'Pass Laws' were introduced, restricting different categories of blacks as to where, how, and for how long they could work.

Three legal categories of black worker were identified. Firstly, preference was given to workers who qualified under stringent 'influx control' laws to live permanently on farms or in the towns, mainly to provide labour in small colonial businesses. Secondly, migrant workers from the reserves in southern and central Namibia usually had to take whatever work they were given. With extreme difficulty a few could gain the legal right to settle permanently at their place of work. This category of worker was principally used to augment the settled labour force in the towns and ranches. Thirdly, the worst-off category were the 'contract workers' (so called because in order to work at all they had to sign an indenture depriving them of all rights).

'Contract workers' were drawn from the northern labour reserves originally to work in the mines and state utilities, but were later used for all manner of menial work. The 'contract labour' category exploited the extreme poverty of thousands, and provided a great reserve army of labour. These workers were available to fill any gaps not covered by the other two categories, and paid so little that they undercut every other section of black labour, ensuring that all categories came cheap. 'Contract workers' were completely unable to secure residency rights in white areas, and so they were always separated from their families when employed.

Pass Laws, ensuring that black workers had to obtain a maze of official permits in order to be able to live or work anywhere outside the labour reserves, were the main instrument of control. They restricted movement and even the freedom to look for work. The general Pass Law was the **Native Administration Proclamation no. 11** of 1922 which ordered that, *"A native found beyond the confines of a location, reserve, farm or place of residence or employment shall exhibit on demand to the police his pass and on neglect to produce may be arrested."*

The **Natives (Urban Areas) Proclamation** of 1924 imposed a more comprehensive and detailed set of controls on workers in the towns and mines. Other laws provided additional restrictions in particular industries, notably the **Mines and Works Proclamation** of 1917 in mining, and the **Masters and Servants Proclamation** of 1920 in farming. By requiring that all blacks outside the reserves should have state-registered jobs, the laws ensured that blacks were only allowed to stay in the designated white areas for as long as they served the labour needs of the employers. All workers had to have 'service contracts', usually for 12 to 18 months at a time, and so the migrant labour system was perpetuated. Most blacks, forced by poverty to find work in white areas, could not settle there with their families. Instead, they had to leave their families in the impoverished rural reserves, returning to join them only when their service contracts ran out and they became unemployed again.

If the majority of migrant workers were badly off, the 'contract workers' from the north were particularly oppressed. Their only choice was whether or not to apply to SWANLA (the South West African Native Labour Association), the semi-official labour recruiting organisation set up in 1926 by the big mines. SWANLA indentures meant that workers had to sign on for periods of 12 to 18 months. They had no right to give notice, and on completion of their contract they had to return to the labour reserve.

Punitive measures against workers gave white employers police-like powers over black workers. A Vagrancy Law was introduced so that blacks could be punished for leaving their designated areas except to work for a white, and the Masters and Servants Proclamation made 'desertion' a criminal offence.

Widespread protest against the migrant labour system led to a general strike in 1971/72 which was started by 'contract' workers. This was brutally repressed by the South African police and army.[13] However, it resulted in the abolition of SWANLA which was replaced by a system of labour bureaux run by the tribal authorities in the 'homelands'.[14]

In 1977, the Administrator-General repealed sections of the Pass Laws thus allowing blacks to stay in urban areas without limit and abolishing the carrying of passes. However, the **Identification of Persons Act**, introduced in 1979, partly replaces the Pass Laws by requiring all adult Namibians to carry an identity card which enables the security forces to check on people's movements.

Major constraints on the free movement of migrant workers are still in operation. They are still obliged to have their work contracts registered, and employers risk a fine if they fail to comply. Moreover, the lack of government provision for urban social services and totally inadequate housing in the towns are the main reasons why workers are prevented from bringing their families to settle with them at their place of work.[15]

The **Abolishment of Racial Discrimination (Urban Areas and Public Amenities) Act** of 1979 opened all urban residential areas and public amenities to all races. This could have been interpreted as an encouraging step, but as one black woman farmer put it, *"Apartheid is about losing your rights and being poor, not about being able to eat in the same restaurants as whites."* [16]

The constitutional changes introduced in 1980 under Proclamation AG8, by allowing the white population group a 'representative authority', ensure that health and education services remain segregated along racial lines because each 'representative authority' is responsible for health and education services for its own 'population group'.

Trade Unions

Labour relations in Namibia are governed by the **Wages and Industrial Conciliation Ordinance** of 1952 which excludes the largest group of black workers, those employed on farms and in domestic service. In 1978 this law was amended to permit blacks to join and form their own trade unions. However, the new legislation contained political restrictions, making it illegal for a registered trade union to assist or affiliate to any political party. Also no trade union may receive funds or assistance from a political party. It is widely held that this legislation was intended to curtail the activities of the main union for blacks, the National Union of Namibian Workers, which was formed in 1978 and is affiliated to SWAPO.

At the end of 1985, the **Wages and Conciliation Amendment Bill** was hastily drawn up reportedly to prevent the employees at Consolidated Diamond Mines from affiliating with the South African National Union of Mineworkers.[17]

Poverty

While the underpaid labour of black men has fuelled the colonial economy, the unpaid labour of black women has underwritten it. The women of migrant labourers' families struggle in the impoverished rural 'homelands' to bring up the next generation of labourers, and to care for the old, discarded generation. Unable to earn even a subsistence in the 'homelands', rural women have to depend on the often insecure remittances of their menfolk. Those who receive none become destitute.

Johanna, a woman of 45 living in a dusty rural settlement in central Namibia, is typical. She is bringing up ten children, all under 12, by herself. She does this by begging food from her neighbours, all of whom are themselves very poor.

"My life is terribly hard. Long ago, my husband went to Windhoek to look for work, but he is unemployed so he never sends money. I get a relief ration from the government each month of beans, maize, jam and fat but it only lasts us for 4 days, so I live by begging for the rest of the month. I send the children out to beg small amounts of food from my neighbours but tonight they came back with nothing, so they will have to

go to bed crying for food. If I cook the small amount of maize porridge I have now, then there would be nothing to give them tomorrow. When we can, we eat porridge for breakfast, but I don't give any to the school-age children because they get a meal at school. Then we have some porridge for lunch, but we rarely eat an evening meal because, if I have to choose, it is better for the children to be asleep when they're hungry. There is no work for me around here, and I cannot leave the children to look for work as I am quite alone." [18] Johanna had wanted a small garden beside the nearby river, but others got to the limited space first.

Susanna Smith

Johanna and some of her children. "I live by begging."

Mass poverty forces tens of thousands of black workers to leave their homes in the rural reserves in search of work as migrant labourers. Although the law, in a technical sense, no longer forces families apart, the general conditions of life for blacks continue to do so. Low wages, high unemployment, the lack of social amenities and a desperate shortage of urban housing, keep men apart from their families. Thousands have tried to reunite their households in the numerous shanty towns growing up around urban centres.

Precise figures are impossible to calculate, but roughly 20% of the black labour force is wholly unemployed and many more are under-employed on the land or in seasonal, short-term work in the towns, fisheries and on white farms.

Migration to the urban areas has been exacerbated by the severe drought which has affected Namibia since 1978, and which has made survival in the 'homelands' even more precarious.

In Windhoek, the spacious white suburbs are placed well apart from the high-density poor townships of Katatura and Khomasdal, reserved for

29

'blacks' and 'coloureds' respectively. About 70,000 people live in Katatura township, which is situated seven miles from the city centre. The bus service is unreliable and expensive, so long lines of workers walking to and from the city can be seen early each morning and late into the evening.

A church social worker in Katatura explained:

"Malnutrition is a very great problem here. It is especially bad in the overcrowded sections of Katatura because these are where the poorest families live. The so-called 'single quarters' are the worst. These were originally built by the municipal authorities for single male migrant workers, but now they are occupied by whole families with no extra rooms or facilities to cope with the increased numbers. Malnutrition is most common amongst children whose parents are unemployed. And much of the malnutrition is hidden from sight because many children, who cannot be fed by their families here, are sent to stay with relatives in the rural areas to relieve the pressure. But we know that they are no better off there." [19]

Susanna Smith

Inside the 'single quarters' of Katutura. Mary, her husband, two children and a lodger live in this one room. "I put up a curtain so we could have a little privacy."

Many mothers are forced to abandon their children because they just cannot afford to feed them. A typical example is Franz, who was abandoned at a community crèche in Katatura. *"We think he's about two years old,"* explained one of the crèche workers. *"His mother left him with us 5 weeks ago saying she would be back in half an hour. She never came back, so now he lives here. He feels the crèche is his home now, that's why he's standing in front of the other children for your photo."* [20]

Two-year-old Franz, standing in front of the other children, was abandoned by his mother who couldn't afford to keep him.

Many other children are not so lucky. The social worker continued, *"We're living in a city where women abandon their babies in dustbins. I've come across many cases of this. It is directly caused by poverty, not lack of compassion."*

The widespread social dislocation in Namibia caused by poverty and migrant labour also takes its toll in the towns.

"We estimate that about 70% of the families in Katatura are one-parent families, many of them headed by unmarried mothers. In 1983, there were 332 baptisms at our local church, and only 16 of these babies were born to married parents."

The same social worker continued, *"Alcoholism and prostitution are also symptoms of the pressures on people here, and I am particularly concerned about the increasing numbers of children turning to drink and prostitution. We find that children suffer psychologically as well as physically from their families' poverty. Young kids are often left alone all day while their mother is out working or looking for work; they grow up in the streets. They have to feed themselves as best they can, that's why you often see children digging in the rubbish tips. There is no proper control by the municipality of the many illicit drinking places in Katatura, so children are free to buy the local home-brewed beer, **Tombo**, which is very strong. We are working with young people who are already alcoholics by the age of 18.*

"Prostitution is the only way many young girls, from the age of 8 upwards, have of surviving. The going price for a child prostitute is R10 (£2.76), while adult prostitutes charge between R20 (£5.50) to R50 (£13.80). So you see, the men, whites and blacks alike, often take the young girls because they are cheaper."

31

Many of the working women in the towns are employed as domestic servants in white households. Aline is a domestic servant in Windhoek who earns R80 (£22) a month, slightly above the average. She explained, *"I am the only breadwinner in my whole family and I support my five children, my parents and my husband. As a result, we all live in poverty"*. While Aline works in Windhoek, her family live in a poor rural settlement in central Namibia.

Aline on a rare visit home to see her children.

"I am not allowed to have my own children with me in Windhoek while I look after my employer's child. I miss my children all the time, and long to see them. But the fare home costs R20 (£5.50), so if I go to see my children, I have even less money to send home for food." [21]

Housing is another major problem for the urban poor: Sofia, a widow since 1980, has five children living with her and has lost three children due to diarrhoea and pneumonia. Her total monthly income is R81 (£22), a widow's pension. The monthly rent she pays for one small room in an overcrowded house is R50 (£14). *"Our room is so small that three of my children have to sleep out here in the backyard."* She pointed to their 'bedroom' — an old car. [22]

Cost of Living

In 1983, a university research team calculated that for minimal survival a black family of six people in Windhoek needed a household subsistence level of R301.48 (£178.68) per month. [23] According to a Windhoek social worker, the average family income in Katatura at the time was R98

(£58).[24] The cost of living is considerably higher in northern Namibia, due to the inflated prices in local shops and stores.

Another 1983 survey found that 86% of black wage earners in Windhoek lived below the household subsistence level, while in the north this applied to 99% of wage earners.[25] The high rate of unemployment and under-employment means that those without paid work have to depend on wage earners already in dire poverty themselves.

Susanna Smith

Three of Sofia's children in front of the broken-down old car which is their bedroom.

Housing in one of Windhoek's white suburbs.

LAND

"When we lost our land, we lost our rights, our family way of life, our independence and our culture." [26] This is how a black woman farmer in central Namibia described the crucial issue of dispossession from the land.

Both the colonial authorities of Germany, prior to 1915, and South Africa wanted Namibia for minerals and for white settler farmers. Both aims required wholesale seizure of land, thereby reducing the area available to peasant production and stock-grazing, and forcing the dispossessed to become wage labourers.

The German authorities began by selective dispossession of some indigenous groups and arranged 'protection treaties' with others. In 1904, the Herero, Damara and Nama peoples of central and southern Namibia rose in protest against German colonial rule. The Germans responded with a ruthless campaign of genocide, killing some 60% of the black population of central and southern Namibia (the so-called 'Police Zone') and nearly all their livestock. [27]

Thereafter, the German regime expropriated nearly all the communal land of these groups. The people of the far north, the Ovambo- and Kavango-speaking peoples, escaped. The Germans feared their military strength, and considered their land as less suitable for white settlement.

The South African colonial authorities took over where the Germans left off. Explicitly linking land and labour policies, they consolidated the former theft of land by creating a two-tier system of labour reserves, which were later to be incorporated into the 'homelands' system.

Blacks in the 'Police Zone' were to provide labour for the white farms and small businesses. The large majority of the black population, in the northern reserves, was regarded as the chief source for migrant labour. In the 1920s the 'contract labour' system was introduced for people in the north, principally those in Ovamboland.

Today, the historical legacy of colonial land expropriation remains intact, with white settler farmers owning the lion's share (77%) of the country's viable farmland.

More than a third of the country's total land surface is desert, or waterless Kalahari **sandveld** (sandy soil). The majority of this barren land has been allocated to the 'homelands'. Of the viable farmland, as much as 90% is dry pasture best suited to stock-farming, and only 10% receives sufficient rainfall to grow crops. Fully 80% of the stock-farming land and half the arable land is occupied by about 5,000 white-owned farms, nearly all of them large ranches. Black farmers and herders are left with fragments of inferior land and desert on the fringes of the white commercial farming zone. Some 40,000 black households struggle to survive on the leftover 20% of the stock-farming zone, and 150,000 peasant households raising livestock and cultivating grain are confined to limited areas of arable land in the far north. The concentration of the black population in the northern 'homelands' means that half the total population are confined to 5% of the viable farmland.[28]

Distribution of viable farmland: average per farming household (hectares)

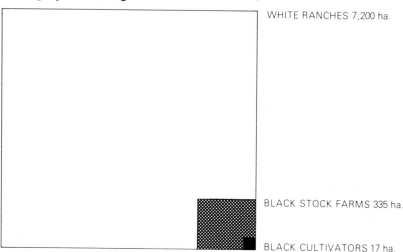

WHITE RANCHES 7,200 ha.

BLACK STOCK FARMS 335 ha.

BLACK CULTIVATORS 17 ha.

The creation of the 'homelands' is the most recent consolidation of previous moves to link labour requirements with land policy. Although some extra land was added to the existing reserves when the 'homelands' were designated, much of the land in the 'homelands' is useless for pastoral or agricultural production.

Proportion of viable farmland in the designated 'homelands' [29]

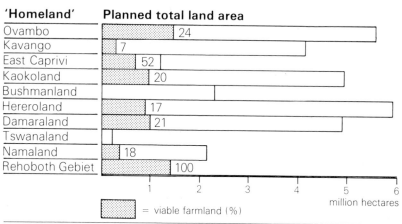

'Homeland'	Planned total land area
Ovambo	24
Kavango	7
East Caprivi	52
Kaokoland	20
Bushmanland	
Hereroland	17
Damaraland	21
Tswanaland	
Namaland	18
Rehoboth Gebiet	100

1   2   3   4   5   6

million hectares

☐ = viable farmland (%)

Susanna Smith

The best farmland is owned by white settlers who raise beef cattle for export.

Agriculture and Food

There are two forms of agriculture in Namibia: the commercial ranching sector which is owned mainly by whites and is export-orientated, and the black agricultural sector which produces mainly for home consumption.

Separate as these two sectors appear, they are nonetheless closely linked by the historical process of land appropriation which has not only reduced black agriculture to today's low levels, but has also forced thousands of impoverished blacks to work as labourers on white farms. In 1983, 50% of the economically active population were employed in black peasant agriculture, and 8% on the commercial farms.[30]

Commercial Agriculture

The white-dominated commercial agricultural sector concentrates on producing beef cattle and karakul sheep almost entirely for export. 92% of the cattle reared are for export to South Africa and 100% of the karakul pelts[31], which are used for manufacturing expensive, high-fashion fur

Heather Hughson

190,000 black peasant families are hardly able to feed themselves on the inferior scraps of land the white settlers didn't want. This child is one of the countless casualties of rural poverty.

37

coats, are exported mainly to the US, Japan and Europe through South Africa.[32]

In 1983, the commercial agricultural sector accounted for 95% of Namibia's marketed agricultural output, 4% of GDP and 12% of total exports.[33]

The export orientation of the commercial agriculture sector, together with the inequitable distribution of wealth and profits earned from the land, raise key issues for Namibia's agricultural economy.

Because so much of the country's land is dry pasture and therefore best suited to stock rearing, a high degree of specialisation is appropriate for ecological reasons. However, the present commercial agricultural sector operates in a highly exploitative manner, particularly with respect to land ownership, employment of labour, and preferential access to government assistance and state-controlled marketing outlets.

As most of the viable farmland is used to rear animals and animal products for export, particularly red meat for South Africa's cities and pelts for the international fur trade, the country is dependent on imports to meet its basic food requirements. Under the present regime, Namibia is a captive market for South African farmers and food marketing companies, importing half its maize requirement and 90% of other foodstuffs.[34] With enough home-produced beef to supply the entire national protein requirement, the majority of Namibians go hungry and many are seriously undernourished. The local food processing industry is so underdeveloped that the consumption of tinned meat is met completely from imports, some of them Namibian products re-exported from South Africa.[35]

For as long as Namibia remains a colony, settler farmers' demands will always take priority over peasant farmers' needs and Namibia's agricultural economy will continue to be geared to South African interests. It is clear that only the attainment of independence will give Namibians the power to begin to transform the present agricultural system by allocating resources to peasant producers and boosting production, as in post-independence Zimbabwe.[36]

As with other sectors of the economy, Namibia's commercial agricultural sector is vulnerable. Due to the extreme dependence on exported produce and imported machinery and goods, the effects of recession are biting hard. In addition, the drought which has affected Namibia since 1978 has seriously harmed commercial and peasant agricultural production. The commercial ranches are reported to be increasingly dependent on state subsidy.[37]

Many white farmers are leaving, frightened of bankruptcy and the possibility of black majority rule. In January 1985 the Administration for Whites doubled its subsidy to prevent white farmers from leaving their farms.[38] Clearly many white farmers would be unlikely to survive even limited agricultural reforms, and this poses problems for the future. Since the whole land issue is so central to the present economy and to the political grievances of the majority, an incoming post-independence government is likely to be faced with a dilemma. On the one hand, the electorate will expect a redistribution of land and more equitable agricultural employment. On the other, the almost exclusive concentration of managerial and marketing skills amongst the white farming population will mean a hiatus at least and, at worst, serious capital flight with possible destruction of fixed assets as white farmers leave Namibia.[39]

Thus the commercial agricultural sector currently brings little benefit to the majority, and is likely to pose serious problems for the future nation.

Farm Labourers

Under the present system, black farm labourers are amongst the most exploited of Namibia's people. The commercial farm labour force is mostly composed of people from the southern and central parts of Namibia. In a white farming area south east of Windhoek, there is a church-run hostel which provides a term-time home for farm labourers' children who live too far away to go to the local school every day. One church worker explained:

"Most farm labourers round here live little better than slaves. They earn about R20 (£5.50) a month plus a fixed food ration, regardless of family size. Work as labourers on the surrounding farms is all that's available. People can hardly survive on the low pay, and, as a result, many of the children we look after at the hostel come to us with malnutrition. The white farmers round here are very hard; most of them do not allow their labourers the 'privilege' of growing a little food on their land. The children we take care of have grown up under oppression, and they don't know anything else but a life of poverty. They will only realise life can be different if they travel and see other things." [40]

Peasant Agriculture

Black agricultural production for household or local market consumption contributes 3% of GDP, reflecting the poor, insufficient land and the near total absence of government assistance available to peasant farmers.[41] 70% of the black population live in the rural areas, depending partly or wholly on agriculture for their income.[42] Altogether, 90% of the population spend at least part of their lives on the land, particularly in childhood and old age.[43]

Peasant farming varies in different parts of the country. In the northern **sandveld** area where the majority of the black population lives, both livestock and crops (principally sorghum and millet) are raised. In the southern part of the country there is insufficient rain for crops so people concentrate on small livestock (sheep and goats), and depend largely on their meagre cash incomes for food.

The San people — also known as 'Bushmen' — who live in the north-eastern part of the country, on the Kalahari **sandveld**, are perhaps the worst off of all Namibia's dispossessed people. Successive enforced reductions of the land available to them, and more recently the drought, have largely destroyed their hunting/gathering subsistence. Poverty and destitution have forced many San into the South African army in Namibia. An estimated 5,000 San soldiers and their families are encamped around the army base at Omega, dependent on the South African presence for their survival. Others live in the slums around Tsumkwe, dependent on government handouts and support from relatives in the army.[44] Many others have survived by working as labourers on white farms (for as little as R9 (£3) a month in 1985[45]), especially during the dry season when traditional foods are in short supply.

Black peasant agriculture is in a state of crisis. The over-crowding and resultant soil degradation arising from apartheid social engineering gets worse as time goes on. Almost no government assistance with credit, inputs, veterinary services, and marketing is available to blacks, in contrast to the enormous farm subsidies and state-controlled services available to white farmers. In 1983, government drought relief totalled R37m (£22m), of which only R6m (£3.5m) went to the 190,000 black peasant households in the country.[46]

With no resources to regenerate their over-used, eroded land, rural people see the inevitable decline of its productivity. A black woman farmer explained:

"We really want to make a living from our land because it is our only hope for the future. But the local government won't give us any help to sink a borehole, and the drought means that now we can't grow anything or water animals without one. Our land is all we have to leave to our children, but it's becoming barren." [47] To add insult to injury, the 'representative authority' responsible for each area levies a poll tax from local people.

Thousands of rural families, especially those without their menfolk, are completely destitute. Paulina, a young single woman living in central Namibia with a 3-month-old baby son explained her problems:

"I don't have any income, my parents are dead, and the father of my child has disappeared. I have no animals, and there is no work around here for me. Often I don't eat from one day to the next. My baby is sick and I'm very worried. Some days my baby just has water from the stream. I get no help from the government." [48]

Until the land tenure system and the present agricultural economy are transformed, there can be no hope for people like Paulina. As she put it, *"When we get independence, I hope I will be able to be independent too with a few cattle and some land for them to graze. Then I will be able to feed my baby."*

Paulina and her sick baby. "He is all I have. I wish I could afford to feed him properly."

MINING AND MINERALS

Most of Namibia's wealth is based on its rich deposits of diamonds, uranium ore and base metals, principally copper, lead, lithium, pyrite, tin, silver and zinc.

The mining sector is owned by South African and western transnational corporations, and by combinations of South African state corporations with western transnationals.[49] The three main mining concerns in Namibia are **Consolidated Diamond Mines (CDM)** owned by De Beers, which is part of the South African Anglo-American group; **Rössing Uranium Ltd**, owned partly by Britain's Rio Tinto Zinc (RTZ) with other shareholdings held by French, Canadian, West German, and South African corporations, and **Tsumeb Corporation Ltd (TCL)** owned by Gold Fields of South Africa, the American firm Newmont Mining Corporation, the British firms Selection Trust Ltd & BP Minerals, and the South African companies O'okiep Copper Company and General Mining Union Corporation, Ltd. (GENCOR).[50]

By the late 1970s, minerals accounted for nearly half of Namibia's GDP, four times more than all agricultural products[51], but the recent recession has brought the proportion of GDP derived from minerals down to 24% in 1983.[52]

Minerals make up a massive 85% of Namibia's total exports[53] and virtually 100% of mineral production leaves the country.[54] However, in spite of the mining industry's crucial importance to the economy, the majority of poor Namibians derive almost no benefit from these national riches. Mining provides relatively few jobs, giving direct employment to 3% of the economically active population.[55] Moreover most of the workforce are migrant workers, who must live separated from their families. Of the total employed in the mining sector in 1983, some 3,200 were white, 13,000 'black' (over 90% migrants) and 800 'coloured'. In the mining industry overall, average wage rates for 1983 were R18,000 (£10,668) for whites, R5,000 (£2,568) for 'blacks', and R9,000 (£5,334) for 'coloureds'.[56]

Because of the high proportion of mineral earnings which are exported, the mining sector largely accounts for the divergence between Namibia's GDP and its GNP.

During the 1982 to 1983 period, nearly a third of the total sales income

Breakdown of total sales income (minerals) 1982 – 83 [57]

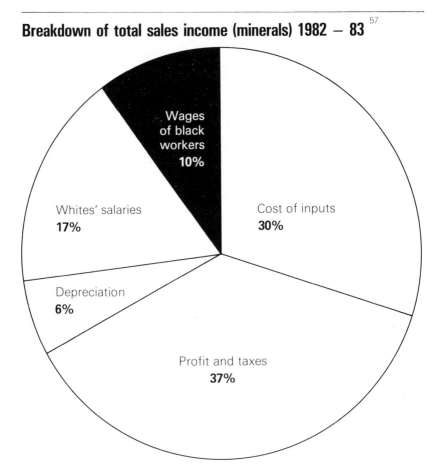

Wages of black workers 10%

Whites' salaries 17%

Cost of inputs 30%

Depreciation 6%

Profit and taxes 37%

from minerals was used to buy inputs which were mainly imported. This expenditure did little to stimulate Namibia's undeveloped local manufacturing base or to provide jobs for the unemployed. It is estimated that over a third of revenue was taken as profit and taxes on profit. As taxes are paid to the South African-controlled administration in Namibia, black Namibians have no democratic say in how these taxes are spent. Of total earnings from sales, as little as one tenth is estimated to have been paid out in wages to the black workforce. Moreover the mining sector's dependence on exports of both raw or minimally processed minerals, and the importance of mining to the national economy makes the industry, and therefore the whole economy, vulnerable to fluctuating world prices. The contribution of mining to GDP has fallen dramatically since 1980, mainly as a result of world recession. As a result, employment in the mines fell from 21,000 in 1977 to 15,000 in 1984.[58]

FISHING

The sea off Namibia's coast contains a plentiful variety of marine life and in pre-colonial times, fish provided an important source of protein for small communities near the shallow coastal lagoons of the Namib desert.[59]

From the late 18th century onwards, foreign fishing interests — starting with European and North American vessels — were attracted to Namibian waters.[60] Then, early this century, a more systematic South African exploitation of Namibia's marine resources developed, severely depleting the rock lobster and the pilchard stocks. With the advent of factory ships in the 1960s, foreign fishing companies could trawl the offshore species unfettered by the South West Africa Administration's flimsy conservation measures. This new technical capacity effectively separated inshore and offshore fishing into today's two distinct industries.

The inshore industry contributed 10% to GDP, and accounted for 10 — 15% of the value of all exports during the mid-70s.[61] However, unchecked over-fishing depleted fish stocks and profits alike and by the end of the 1970s the contribution to GDP had fallen to 2%, plus another 1% from processing.[62] After a slight recovery, the contribution to GDP in 1983 was approximately 9%.[63]

Most of the inshore catch is exported, mainly to South Africa, which ensures its own preferential access to the market. The result is that most Namibians cannot benefit from this valuable source of protein. The inshore industry provides approximately 1% of total employment, plus another 1% during the peak season. [64] However its collapse in the late 1970s due to over-fishing has meant that five out of the nine processing factories have closed down, and two- thirds of the workers employed in the mid-70s have lost their jobs.[65]

Inshore fishing is largely carried out by vessels owned by white businessmen and run by black crews. Six South African companies, based principally at Walvis Bay, own the inshore processing industry (tinning, plus oil or meal extraction). During the boom of the mid-70s, profits were high and companies could recover the entire cost of their investments within three or four years.[66] Gross company profits were estimated to have been as high as R50m (£31.8m) with only R8m (£5.09m) going on wages, food and rent to the 7,000 black workers.[67] The profits mostly left the country, either as dividends and soft loans to shareholders or to be invested abroad, as the decline in pilchard stocks became apparent.

The high rate of return on capital and the size of profits dropped as sales plummeted, but the companies involved have not been hurt by their over-fishing as they have diversified and have invested their profits elsewhere, mostly in South Africa.[68] Taxes to the South African-controlled administration in Namibia have averaged 30 − 35% of gross profits in recent years, a rate estimated to be low by world standards.[69]

The offshore, foreign-dominated industry has also over-exploited fish stocks and absolutely no benefit accrues to Namibia from this industry. The bulk of the offshore catch goes to the USSR and Eastern European countries.

Without its own national government, Namibia has not been able to secure an internationally accepted exclusive economic zone, so the offshore factory ships are free to come and go at will. The South African-appointed Administrator- General for Namibia proclaimed a 370km fishery zone to be in force in April 1981. But due to the illegality in international law of South Africa's occupation of Namibia, this zone has been regarded as null and void by the long-distance factory trawlers. The United Nations Council for Namibia (UNCN) has signed the Law of the Sea Convention on Namibia's behalf, but has not yet proclaimed a 370km zone.[70]

A voluntary body acting as a regional fishery convention for Namibia, the International Commission for the South-East Atlantic Fisheries (ICSEAF), was formed in 1969 by most of the states who fish these waters, principally the USSR, Eastern European countries, Spain and South Africa. Its main functions are to provide a forum for the member governments to agree regulatory measures and to organise back-up, monitoring and information services.[71]

The UNCN has no representative on the ICSEAF, and although the South African-controlled administration is represented, South African fishing companies are less concerned with conserving Namibia's wealth for the future than they are with their own profits. Thus the ICSEAF has been called *"not so much a regional convention as an open-ended club of foreign states whose trawlers exploit Namibia's offshore waters"*.[72]

Without a strong national government to safeguard its interests, it is likely that Namibian waters will continue to be over-fished by foreign companies and Eastern European state fleets, and profits and catches will continue to be exported. The future nation will be left with a needlessly run-down inshore industry, dependent on South African finance and expatriate managerial skill, and an export-dominated offshore sector of little benefit to the Namibian economy.[73] The whole industry could continue to by-pass local nutritional and employment needs. In the meantime a precious national asset has been so severely depleted that some species may never recover.

Given that Namibia's economy is overwhelmingly geared towards the interests of settlers and foreign investors, without regard for the needs of the black majority, it is not surprising that in Oxfam's experience development work with poor communities meets with considerable obstacles.

There is an urgent need to transform the structures which cause and perpetuate poverty for the majority. But these structural changes can only begin after independence.

CHAPTER 2

OBSTACLES TO DEVELOPMENT

The obstacles to development work and to the development of the poor majority are immense. Courageous attempts to promote community-based projects in the vital fields of education and training, health, child care, agriculture, water supply and legal aid are however under way. Oxfam, together with other international voluntary agencies, is supporting these initiatives, more because of the present difficulties than in spite of them. As one Namibian development worker put it:

"During the '70s, we used to think that development was something we'd all turn our minds to after independence. Now we realise that we've got to get on with it, so that when independence comes we'll have laid the foundations of our new society. If we just sit and wait, our fear is that when independence finally comes, it will just be independence in a formal, political sense with no real social and economic dimensions." [1] In Oxfam's experience, after 22 years of working in Namibia, the difficulties frustrating community development have clear economic and political causes.

Economically, the majority of Namibians are prevented from climbing out of the pit of poverty and destitution. In general, people do not have adequate land to produce enough for themselves, let alone a surplus with which to generate income. There is no economic base on which to overcome the poverty of the majority, and therefore little chance for community development schemes based on income from agricultural production. In some areas of the country, it may be possible to develop more intensive forms of agricultural production, with the use of irrigation for example. But in general, the pressing need is for more extensive access to land as well as to water resources, agricultural credit and inputs. Only extensive land reforms and state provision for the peasant agricultural sector after independence will begin to resolve this major obstacle to development.

Politically, black Namibians have been marginalised in all areas of life. They cannot exercise basic democratic rights in the shaping of their society. Harsh legislation, the sweeping powers of the security forces, the poor education system available to blacks, and the divisive 'homelands' policy have repressed the emergence of community organisations through which development work should take place.

However, the national liberation movement and the church structures have continued to operate in spite of state repression. Oxfam's principal partners in Namibia are the Anglican, Catholic and Lutheran churches as well as the Council of Churches in Namibia (CCN). With membership made up from the major churches in Namibia, except the Dutch Reformed Church, the CCN's various departments provide a major focus for national, non-governmental organisation development activity. The CCN runs schemes in education and training (including a scholarship programme for Namibians to study overseas), welfare, health, agriculture, water supply, and legal aid. The CCN is also a tireless critic of South Africa's occupation. In January 1986, its offices were seriously damaged by an arson attack.[2]

OXFAM'S ROLE

In the light of the underlying obstacles to development, Oxfam has identified the following objectives for its work inside Namibia:

- to support community-based projects, run by members of those communities, in order to strengthen local confidence in self-help initiatives;
- in a society ravaged by divisive policies, to give special support to cooperative initiatives which aim to overcome these divisions at a local level;
- to give special attention to independent, non-governmental work in education and health. This includes support to:
  - projects which give children access to a balanced school curriculum;
  - projects for popular education which help to strengthen people's organisational skills and their ability to form local community development organisations;
  - projects which promote community health awareness and better health;
- to provide humanitarian assistance, through the churches, to people in special need.

However, the role of an agency like Oxfam is always limited compared with the overall needs of a given country, and in comparison to the impact of national development policies. Oxfam's experience is that, in Namibia's case, the net effect of the state provision for blacks has been to create serious obstacles to development. Furthermore, South Africa's military occupation of northern Namibia has had devastating consequences for development work, for the provision of vital services, and for the everyday lives of ordinary people.

EDUCATION

Despite the relaxation of some 'petty apartheid' laws, the education service is firmly segregated along racial lines. The resulting unequal allocation of resources together with the style and content of the curriculum available to blacks are major obstacles to development. The poor state of black education is a direct result of colonial policies to keep black Namibians as second-class citizens. A school teacher in northern Namibia explained:

"We have so many frustrated young people in secondary school. They are clever and able but the poor educational facilities provided for blacks mean they cannot achieve their potential, and their employment prospects under the apartheid system fall far short of their ability. I know that this is why so many young people cross the border in search of a brighter future".[3]

Today, illiteracy amongst black adults runs at 60% and only two-thirds of black primary school leavers are literate.[4] Education for black children is not compulsory, as it is for white children.

Lack of adequate state funding to blacks-only schools means these children have no classroom.

More than five times as much is spent per head on white children's schooling as on black children's.[5] Furthermore, education for white and 'coloured' children is free, whereas 'blacks' have always had to pay for theirs.[6] Although, in comparison to other black workers, black school teachers are well paid, they are poorly trained in comparison to white teachers.

There is a notable lack of state provision for vocational training for blacks, as there is for further education of any sort. Indeed, **only 1%** of black adult Namibians have completed secondary education.[7] The 'Cape syllabus' adopted for use in state schools is heavily biased towards official white South African history, culture and political perspectives.[8]

The main implications of the education system for blacks are listed below. They all create obstacles to development now and have major implications for educational reform in the future.

● The education services for blacks are not only racially separated from services for whites and 'coloureds', but they are also divided according to the 'homelands' system. Thus, each 'representative authority' is nominally responsible for administering the education service in its respective 'homeland'. This underlines the 'divide and rule' policy on which South Africa's political control of Namibia's black population rests.

The entire 'homelands' policy, and the political premise on which it is based, is fundamentally incompatible with independence and democratic social development. In the words of one Namibian educationalist, *"Education in the fullest sense, in the sense of broadening the mind and realising a child's potential, cannot possibly be achieved under the present system"*.[9]

● The choice of language in schools is an important issue for Namibians. After Afrikaans, English and German also rank as official languages in Namibia, but Afrikaans is the main teaching medium used in primary and secondary schools. Although Afrikaans is the mother tongue of some black Namibians, it is seen by most as the language of their oppressors. Afrikaans thus has cultural and political connotations which offend the black majority, and because it has no international currency it also, according to the United Nations Institute for Namibia, *"serves as an instrument of isolation and insularity"*.[10] Consequently, an important plank of SWAPO's post-independence educational policy is to promote English as the main official language, while also appreciating the importance of indigenous languages including Afrikaans. At present English is poorly taught in black schools.

● State education services for blacks are designed to equip children with only the minimum skills necessary for the existing economy and political structures. As a result, only 22% of black children go on to higher primary school (according to 1980 figures), and only 1% of black adults complete secondary education.[11] Mathematics and science teaching are inadequate, and non- existent in many secondary schools.

Education for an independent Namibia

It is generally assumed that many of the skilled, white people in Namibia will choose to leave when full independence under a majority government becomes a reality. Namibia's economy and civil service are heavily dependent on white and expatriate people at managerial and technical levels. Many whites are already leaving, taking their skills and assets with them.

To differing extents, this process has taken place in other African countries, many of which are still suffering the long-term effects of attaining independence without the necessary stock of skills and experience to change and run their systems of government and economic life. In Oxfam's experience — in Mozambique for instance — this is one of the harshest colonial legacies.

In Namibia's case, the independent government will need to fill thousands of high and middle level posts left empty by whites. Altogether, on independence an estimated total of over 16,000 middle and high level posts in managerial, professional and skilled categories will need to be filled for effective management of government services and commerce.[12] At the moment, almost 90% of the labour force, and a higher proportion of the total population, have less than complete primary education. Virtually all the 10,000 holders of university, teaching or equivalent in-service qualifications are white.[13]

Add to this the educational demands which Namibian people will feel it their right to make — for compulsory schooling, a balanced syllabus, adult literacy training, the introduction of English as the official national language, decent opportunities for vocational and further education — and the magnitude of the problem is clear. A complete transformation of the present services will be necessary.

Several vitally important non-governmental programmes designed to promote a new kind of education for black Namibians are already under way inside Namibia and amongst Namibia's refugee population. But it should be emphasised that these initiatives remain limited in comparison to the sheer scale of the overall problem.

Inside Namibia, there are a handful of 'independent' schools run by churches to provide *"an education for a free Namibia"* as one headmaster put it.[14] English, mathematics and science subjects are prominent in the independent schools' curriculum. Instead of the 'Cape syllabus' taught in the government schools, they have chosen to use the Lesotho syllabus which has been specially prepared for use in the independent Southern African States. As one teacher in school said, *"The Cape syllabus gives students an unbalanced view of the world. Take the Cape history books for instance. They do not reflect the whole truth about our country's history — instead they concentrate only on the white man's history".*[15]

Another teacher explained the difficulties faced by students who have been through the state school system when they apply for higher education church scholarships abroad:

"Our children in state secondary schools are taught Afrikaans, a little English, their mother tongue, history and bible studies. With that sort of educational background, you don't qualify for further studies anywhere outside. This means that many secondary school leavers train here as teachers, and therefore the next generation of students suffer because

their teachers don't know science, maths and English. Most pupils aren't even advised in school that they need science and maths in order to take up further studies. I work on a church scholarships committee, and I have files full of applications from secondary school leavers who don't qualify. I've seen so many of them crying when they find their examination certificates are no use. They feel cheated and despondent, so many of them cross the border to become refugees in search of a brighter future. The independent schools are providing a vital service — we must have scientists, engineers, doctors and accountants for our future nation. We must break our dependence on the skills and know-how of the whites; we can't be properly independent otherwise." [16]

The Namibia Literacy Programme (NLP) is a non-governmental organisation which has a country-wide network of literacy promoters who work with locally formed classes of adult learners. The NLP produces its own functional literacy materials in all the main Namibian languages. One NLP staff member described the problems they are up against:

"Illiteracy is a serious and widespread problem and that is why we are running this organisation. In a properly independent Namibia, there would be no need for a private organisation to be running a national literacy programme, effectively single-handed; it would be one of the Government's primary responsibilities." [17]

Several important educational schemes for Namibians are also being implemented outside Namibia. In the SWAPO refugee settlements in Angola and Zambia, the education of children and adults alike is high on

SWAPO looks after thousands of pre-school children at this refugee settlement in Angola.

the list of priorities. In contrast to the official education system inside Namibia, every effort is made to prepare school children for life in post-independence Namibia. In SWAPO's refugee settlement in Zambia, for example, a library and a good stock of science equipment are available for the students' use. Science subjects and maths are part of the curriculum, together with Namibian and African history. Pupils are required to go from primary to secondary levels, and as many as possible go on for further training or higher education. English is the teaching medium, and the teachers are black Namibians, most of whom have graduated from the school themselves. Most importantly, school education is compulsory for all the children, and seen as a right.[18]

For the adults at the settlement, literacy classes are held daily both in English and the Namibian languages. Only about 25% of adult refugees are literate in English on arrival in the settlements.[19]

In addition to the education and training activities organised by SWAPO in the settlements, Namibian refugees are also assisted by the United Nations Nationhood Programme set up, *"To provide assistance to Namibians who have suffered from persecution and to finance a comprehensive educational and training programme with particular regard to their future administrative responsibilities"*.[20] The United Nations Institute for Namibia (UNIN) in Zambia's capital, Lusaka, was established in 1976 as part of the UN Nationhood Programme, to train Namibians, *"To form the core of public service managers and administrators for independent Namibia"*. The other major role played by UNIN is to develop and analyse data and strategy which will serve future policy makers and planners in post-independent Namibia.[21]

UNIN relies for its existence on the support of international aid donors, including the British Overseas Development Administration which covers the costs of three English language teachers. The international community also provides educational opportunities for Namibians abroad. British official aid contributes 50 training awards a year, concentrating on training English language teachers and public administrators.[22]

Important as these external services for Namibians are, South Africa's continued illegal occupation means that, for the most part, Namibians must leave their country if they are to benefit from the educational opportunities offered by SWAPO, the UN and bilateral aid donors.

HEALTH

Poverty and poor health

Widespread poor health is perhaps the most debilitating consequence of poverty in Namibia. According to UN figures, the mortality rate for black infants[23] in Namibia is well above average for Africa. In contrast, the mortality rate for white infants is directly comparable to the world's most developed nations. A black baby is over seven times more likely to die in infancy than a white baby.[24]

The main health problems related to poverty and poor living conditions in Namibia are malnutrition, infectious diseases – especially gastroenteritis and tuberculosis – and stress-related health problems.

Malnutrition

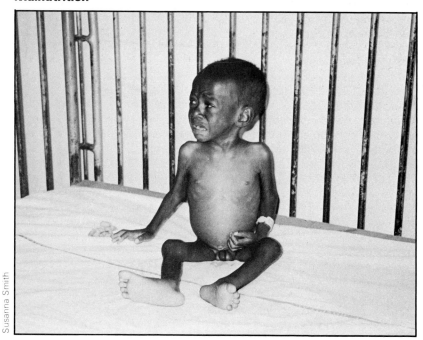

Susanna Smith

Nobody knows how many thousands of black children suffer from malnutrition in Namibia. This little boy is one of the lucky few receiving special feeding in hospital.

Reliable statistics on malnutrition levels have been scant, mainly because virtually no outreach nutritional assessment and surveillance work is done in Namibia. However, experienced health workers suggest that malnutrition is a very serious problem, particularly among young children. Many of Oxfam's partners confirm this. For example, according to a

53

nursing sister on the paediatric ward at a mission hospital in Ovamboland:
"Babies and young children suffering from malnutrition and diarrhoea are our main problem. We try to keep those who reach the hospital alive with therapeutic feeding, but we know that many more are suffering from hunger out in the villages." [25]

A health worker in Katatura (Windhoek's black township) explained:
"Child malnutrition is a very serious problem here in town, as well as in the rural areas. Food prices are higher in the 'black' and 'coloured' townships than in Windhoek city centre. The traders take advantage of us because Katatura is so far from the city centre. We are trying to help by promoting back-yard gardening through our community health committee, but basically the hunger is caused by poverty and it won't go away unless people see a big rise in their standard of living.

"A lot of mothers nowadays do not breastfeed because they are out working or looking for work. So they turn to powdered milk which is very expensive at R4 (£1.10) for two days' supply. To eke it out, mothers tend to over-dilute the powder and so the babies become underfed. Many babies are given sugar water or black tea in their bottles instead of milk." [26]

Infectious diseases

Because malnutrition particularly affects young children and their ability to fight infection, the incidence of preventable diseases is alarmingly high amongst under-fives. Poor living conditions, particularly overcrowded housing and inadequate sanitation, serve to increase the risk of infection.

According to Windhoek statistics, 'black' infants are 40 times more at risk of dying from meningitis, gastroenteritis or tuberculosis than white infants.[27] 'Coloured' infants are in between, about 26 times more at risk than white infants. Gastroenteritis alone accounts for the same number of deaths among 'coloured' infants per 1,000 live births as are accounted for by all causes of death among white infants. Among 'black' infants, twice this number die from gastroenteritis alone.[28] The national incidence of gastroenteritis is unknown since community health surveys are not routinely undertaken, and only the most severely affected black children within reach of a hospital are taken there, with only the worst cases actually admitted. Among white babies, the situation is entirely different, with the first signs of diarrhoea leading to rapid referral and early admission to hospital.[29]

While diarrhoea is by far the most common illness affecting black children, tuberculosis is the most common amongst black adults.[30] Tuberculosis is a useful indicator of 'development' as it is mainly a disease of poverty and overcrowding. Whereas its incidence has declined in Europe and the USA as a result of improved living standards, in Namibia TB is rampant particularly amongst black migrant workers. It is more common among rural than urban people, much more prevalent among blacks than whites, and more common among migrant workers than settled residents.[31]

TUBERCULOSIS

- In the USA the estimated incidence* of the disease was 1.39 per 10,000 people in 1977.
- In England the incidence was 1.64 per 10,000 people in 1978-79.
- In South Africa, a conservative estimate was 25 per 10,000 people in 1980 with an incidence amongst blacks 15 times that amongst whites.
- In Namibia, estimates of incidence vary between 40 and 500 per 10,000 people, with blacks being up to 50 times more at risk than whites.[32]

* Incidence = number of new cases each year

Sleeping sickness, malaria, tick fever, bilharzia, typhoid, diphtheria, tetanus, whooping cough, polio, hepatitis, leprosy, VD, eye infections and scabies are among the other infectious diseases which particularly affect blacks because they relate to poverty and poor health services.

Stress-related health problems

The stress of being poor in a violent and divided society has serious effects on people's health and well-being.

Mental health

Health services for blacks are so underdeveloped that there are no official statistics on the incidence of mental illness amongst blacks, only a handful of psychiatric beds in the general wards of Katatura and Caprivi hospitals, and no black psychiatrists or psychiatric nurses.[33] However, it is clear from Oxfam's contacts with social workers that mental problems related to stress are significant.

A widow in Katatura with five children explained: *"I have so many problems trying to feed my children and keep a roof over our heads that often I just sit and cry. I feel like running away from everything".*[34]

A Namibian social worker focusing on women's problems in Katatura reports:

"When talking of Katatura, one is inevitably talking about women along certain ethnic/tribal lines because of the apartheid layout of the township itself, and this segregation imposes serious limitations on normal contact between people. People live in separate worlds as far as their life experiences are concerned, even though they are subjected to the same constraints, such as overcrowding, lack of privacy, not to mention callous treatment at the municipal rental offices and the Katatura hospital. As a result of this divided, harsh way of life I have often noticed that women in Katatura suffer stress-related complaints, such as heart palpitations, headaches, faintness and anxiety . . . Many women are constantly moving from reserve to reserve, from reserve to townships, and even in the townships they shift from house to house staying with different relatives, their lives are restless and anxious . . . Many women turn towards the 'healing churches', and one church prophetess told me,

'Her children are hungry, they want clothing but the woman has no money. She thinks and thinks and worries about this all the time, until she becomes mentally unbalanced. By the time she comes to our church, she needs help'.'' [35]

Katatura, the township for blacks outside Windhoek, is divided up into 'tribal' sections to prevent unity amongst blacks. This woman's front door is stamped with an 'O' to denote that she lives in the 'Ovambo' section.

Susanna Smith

Alcoholism

"People turn to drink because they are anxious and there is nothing for them to hope for", said a Katatura social worker. ***"Tombo** houses are open from dawn until late at night serving strong, home-brewed beer. It only costs 10 cents (3p) for a half litre so it's one of the few things the poor can afford."* [36]

According to reports given at an international seminar in 1983 on health in Namibia, alcoholism has reached very serious proportions, with some 50% of adults in Katatura, and 80% of adults in Khomasdal (the 'black' and 'coloured' townships outside Windhoek) reported to be alcoholics.[37]

An independent researcher studying urbanisation in Namibia reports: *"Although not officially admitted or documented, alcoholism has rapidly reached epidemic proportions, directly or indirectly affecting roughly 50% of Katatura and Khomasdal adults. Shebeens are ubiquitous, and expenditure on alcohol is high. A one-month survey of patients . . . by a doctor practising in Katatura and Khomasdal substantiated these claims."* [38]

Poor health will continue to be a major obstacle to development in Namibia for as long as its causes — the economic, social and political structures which marginalise the black majority — exist. Until Namibian society is transformed, health services as such will not significantly reduce the existing health problems. It is nonetheless worth examining the existing health services in Namibia because, in their present form, they compound the problems of inequality in health, and present a pressing case for a new national health policy for an independent Namibia.

Organisation of health services

As is the case with the state education services, apartheid is apparent at two levels in the provision of health services. Firstly, they are racially segregated, and secondly the administration of health services for blacks in the rural areas has been given over to the separate, second-tier, 'representative authorities'.

An entirely disproportionate amount of health resources are allocated to whites, as the following state expenditure figures show:

Per Capita Spending on Health Services (1981) [39]

'Representative Authority'	Total Spending per Person
Rehoboth	R 4.70
Damara	R 15.02
Ovambo	R 24.85
Caprivi	R 37.06
Kavango	R 56.84
Whites	R233.70

The town of Okahandja, north of Windhoek, illustrates the unequal access to health care. In 1981 it had a population of 13,320 blacks and 1,800 whites. For the whites there was a twelve-bed hospital with facilities for general surgery, maternity, and chronic and infectious diseases. There were also X-ray facilities and the hospital was run by a medical superintendent. For blacks there was no hospital, only a four-bed clinic run by a nursing sister. This gives a ratio of one bed for 150 whites, compared with one bed for 3,330 blacks.[40]

While whites receive the benefits of expensive medical technology, blacks do not. A new clinical block of the Windhoek State Hospital, opened in 1982, boasts some of the most modern equipment in Africa. In contrast, at a state-aided mission hospital for blacks in Ovamboland, an Oxfam visitor noted that the baby clinic had run out of weight cards, and the dispensary was very short of several essential drugs.[41]

The wide disparity in expenditure between white and black hospital facilities was highlighted by a report in the *Windhoek Observer* in April 1985 claiming that Namibia had built the most expensive hospital in the world, at a cost of R1m (£413,000) per bed. The paper reported that the Keetmanshoop State Hospital for whites had never had more than 23 patients, so small is the white population it caters for. By contrast, Onandjukwe hospital for blacks in Ovamboland is desperately overcrowded with 250 beds officially but, according to one staff member, *"always a minimum of 400 in-patients".* [42] A new paediatric block has recently been built but there are no funds to open it.

In the 'homelands' as a whole, the most optimistic doctor to population

Susanna Smith

This desperately needed paediatric block at a blacks-only hospital cannot be opened for lack of state funds.

ratio in 1980 was about 1:12,000,[43] compared to the ratio in Zambia that year of 1:7,670.[44] There are almost no black doctors, and no medical training facilities. The health service is very dependent on the skills of white personnel, many of whom are expected to leave if a black majority government comes to power.[45]

Orientation of the health services

In its health work worldwide, Oxfam gives special emphasis to the Primary Health Care approach of which the essential features are that:
- the promotion of health depends fundamentally on improving socio-economic conditions and on the elimination of poverty and under-development;
- the mass of people should participate as well as benefit from this process;
- the delivery of basic curative and preventive health care should be at community level, and should respond to local people's overall needs.

The structure and orientation of existing health services in Namibia, (state, mission and private), are quite at odds with this model. The Council of Churches in Namibia (CCN) is organising a health programme which aims to provide a new approach. Health committees, made up of local people, have been organised in various poor communities. Committee meetings are held regularly, and participants have the chance to discuss health and development issues from their own perspective. After full, participatory discussions it is envisaged that community health activities will be agreed and organised by local people. This programme is embryonic, but represents a very small ray of hope in a system that is otherwise biased towards curative, secondary, urban facilities.

Curative services receive the lion's share of health resources. Less than 2% of overall health expenditure is spent on preventive services.[46] Furthermore, most recent health expenditure has been on new buildings for curative medicine. This means that an increasing proportion of health expenditure in the future will have to be spent on their maintenance and staffing. The health service after independence will thus be heavily mortgaged against preventive services.

For white people, most of whom live in or near towns, access to health services is not a problem. But scattered black rural populations are often far away from health services. A survey among Namibian refugees revealed that about 70% of schools were more than 10km away from a health, centre, while 5% of schools were more than 100km away from health facilities. In many cases, people's homes were even further away, since hospitals and schools tend to be sited together, particularly on mission stations.[47] Although well over half of the black population lives in the 'homelands', less than 20% of doctors work there. Moreover less than 20% of health resources are spent in the 'homelands', reflecting the white, urban bias of the health services.[48]

The government of independent Namibia will be faced with the enormous task of eliminating these racial inequalities in the provision of health care, and in making the orientation of health services appropriate to the needs of the majority. But its major task will be to eradicate the poverty which is the principal cause of the appallingly poor health in Namibia.

MILITARY OCCUPATION

The war between SWAPO and the South African Defence Force (SADF) has been going on for twenty years. It started in 1966, in the same year that the UN General Assembly revoked South Africa's mandate.

An estimated 100,000 SADF troops occupy Namibia; approximately one soldier to every 15 civilians.[49] This makes Namibia one of the most intensively occupied countries in the world.[50] The effects have been devastating. The everyday lives of the peasant communities in the north have been seriously disrupted, as have basic services such as health and education. Community development efforts in the war zone have been almost totally destroyed. A school teacher in the militarised zone describes the effects of military occupation: *"The war makes our people even poorer. All the local farmers round here live in fear. They are frequently questioned at gunpoint and sometimes beaten up. Every day there is something. The soldiers often drive their heavy vehicles over people's crops, just for the sake of it. What can we do?"* [51]

One of the principal strategies of the occupying forces is to prevent civilian assistance to SWAPO guerrillas by using harsh 'counter insurgency' measures. For the local people, this usually means intimidation and harassment, but many cases of torture, murder, rape and the destruction of crops and homes have also been reported and documented over the years.[52]

Thus, the occupying army's 'front line' is, effectively, the small wood and thatch villages dotted throughout the northern countryside and their targets include the local peasant population. There is a dawn to dusk curfew and anyone breaking it risks being shot on sight.

It is widely held that there will be no military solution to the war, and that only a political settlement can bring an end to the death, suffering and destruction it brings. The war itself exacerbates poverty and frustrates development, as indicated by reports from Oxfam's partners in the war zone, all underlining the need for an early settlement.

At Onekwaya, a small settlement in Ovamboland, there is an independent mission school which has been seriously affected by the war over the years. In the first place the school was forced to move from its former buildings at Odiibo right on the Angolan border where much of the fighting takes place, because of the security risks to the children and staff. A teacher at the school said, *"But even after the move we continue to be troubled. The South African soldiers disrupt our work and make us afraid for the safety of our children. For example, they often just burst into the classrooms, without asking any of us in charge, and they question the children roughly. They harass the girls. They shoot into the air to frighten us. Our lives and work are made very difficult, and the children are scared."* [53]

The Evangelical Lutheran Ovambo-Kavango Church in Namibia (ELOC), carries out a variety of development projects which have been badly disrupted by the war. Their printing press at Oniipa has twice been destroyed by bombs, and on a third occasion the shell failed to explode.

The ELOC printing press after it had been destroyed by South African bombing.

An ELOC worker said, *"We used the press for printing a church magazine for the local community, school text books, children's weight charts for the local hospital, and hymn books."* [54]

An independent ELOC secondary school in Oshigambo, near the Angolan border, has also been badly hit. A staff member explained: *"Two of our children have recently been shot and injured by the army. They said it was 'by accident' but they are reckless when they harass us. Our children live in constant fear because the local army base is very close and every week soldiers saunter through the school premises with their guns. It's been like this since 1977."* [55]

In January 1986, a bomb blast destroyed the school's electricity generators. There were no casualties but the damage was estimated at R30,000 (£9,724). An official ELOC statement blames the South African Defence Force. [56]

An ELOC development worker explained the enormous problems he encounters when trying to promote village-level development projects: *"Take for example a village well which Oxfam funded. The local people have very serious problems with their water supply. The soil is so sandy that it is necessary to line wells with concrete, otherwise people must rely on dirty drinking holes frequented by animals. The local authorities refused to help the village make a well because they said the village would give water to the guerillas. So when I started meeting with this village to discuss what they would like to do about their water problems, where they would like to site the well and how they would organise the labour, they were very suspicious of me, and at first they didn't want to talk. You see, the army divides villages by bribing some people to be informers and harassing others. As a result nobody really knows who is on which side, and there is little trust between people. Without trust there can be no development in a community."* [57]

The 'representative authority' for Ovamboland refused to help these villagers sink a well, so they must continue to draw their drinking water from this dirty pond.

The vital mobile health work which used to be carried out from ELOC's Onandjukwe hospital in the war zone was forced to stop in 1982. A hospital staff member explained: *"We had to stop because two of our ambulances were blown up by land mines, the two drivers were killed and the nurses and patients in the ambulance were injured. Our mobile health nurses were constantly being harassed by South African soldiers who are suspicious of anyone who travels about in the rural areas."* [58]

The mobile team's work was vital. They carried out regular immunisation of children under five, regular weighing and health checks of babies, and ante-natal screening for thousands of expectant mothers. The staff member continued, *"We will only be able to start up our mobile work again once the war is ended. We're seeing the results of no mobile services now — more and more children who have not been immunised come to the hospital with preventable diseases like whooping cough, and more come to the cemetery."*

The Namibian Literacy Programme is a voluntary organisation promoting adult literacy. A staff member said: *"Our work is particularly badly affected by the war in the north. You see, many of the people who join our classes there have to walk six or seven kilometres each way. They are afraid of army harassment, land mines or failing to get home before the curfew. Our students and staff are often picked up and interrogated, as the South African army is suspicious of anyone who moves about. One of our instructors, for example, was recently picked up after he'd finished his class. He was detained for two days without his family knowing where he was. It's very hard for our staff to work in these conditions, and our programme suffers as a result."* [59] (NB. In January 1985, the Windhoek office of the Namibian Literacy Programme was damaged by vandals. It has been reported that the attack was politically motivated.[60])

Harassment of civilians by SADF troops, *"is so common it's not even notable"*, said one development worker. *"The army regularly drive their armoured trucks over people's crops, that's why so many people have moved from their original homes — so that they can grow food in peace."* [61]

The Council of Churches in Namibia (CCN) runs a legal aid scheme to help the victims of South African army harassment and physical abuse. The doctor responsible for examining plaintiffs of the CCN scheme said, *"People are now coming forward more and more with their complaints, even though it is a long and difficult business for ordinary peasants to take the army to court. But they are doing it, they've had enough."* [62]

In the war zone, the numerous South African army bases have become part of the scenery. An army gun turret overlooks a graveyard in Ovamboland.

CHAPTER 3

BRITISH RESPONSIBILITIES

For over a century, Britain has been closely connected with Namibia, both directly and through its deep-rooted connections with South Africa. The strength of these links with Namibia and South Africa places a particularly heavy responsibility on the British Government to press for change.

DIPLOMATIC AND POLITICAL LINKS

As both a Contact Group member and a permanent member of the United Nations Security Council, Britain is particularly well placed to help break the present stalemate.

The Contact Group has failed in its objective to secure Namibia's independence through implementation of SC Resolution 435. Indeed, latterly, Britain has been seen to be taking a soft line in its attitude towards the US policy of 'linkage' to the issue of the Cuban military presence in Angola. Having voted, (in October 1983) for Resolution 539, rejecting 'linkage', the British Government's position appears to have shifted. Current policy is not to reject 'linkage' unequivocally, but rather to accommodate the South African Government's insistence on it as a guiding factor in determining British policy. In view of this accommodation of South Africa's position, a recent Government policy paper states: *"We therefore consider that, in practice, US- led negotiations on Cuban withdrawal offer a prospect of progress towards implementation of Security Council Resolution 435"*.[1]

Britain's role in the UN Security Council is vital, along with that of two other Contact Group states, the United States and France, who are also permanent members of the Security Council.[2] In blocking numerous Security Council resolutions on Namibia calling for economic sanctions against South Africa, British economic interests in both countries are protected.

The voting record of successive British Governments at the UN Security Council demonstrates a clear division between adherence to the principle of Namibia's independence, and evasion of any international action to press for the achievement of that independence which might harm British financial interests in Namibia and South Africa. (See Appendix 1 for list of UN Security Council Resolutions on Namibia and Britain's voting pattern.)

INTERNATIONAL LAW

South Africa's illegal occupation of Namibia and international inaction

In spite of the overwhelming consensus that South Africa's occupation of Namibia is illegal, expressed by the International Court of Justice in 1971 and since then by innumerable UN resolutions, the decision to take action against South Africa has been consistently evaded by the major world powers most closely involved in Namibia.

The UK, the USA and France have all used their power of veto in the Security Council to prevent the UN from taking effective action.

A brief outline of the international legal debate over Namibia shows that Britain, along with other permanent members of the Security Council, needs to generate a new political will if the UN is to be able to discharge its responsibility for Namibia effectively.

When the UN was established in 1945, following the collapse of the League of Nations, all countries administering League of Nations mandates agreed to enter into trusteeship agreements with the UN — with the exception of South Africa. These agreements were intended to lead to the granting of full independence to the mandated territories. South Africa refused to enter into a trusteeship agreement over Namibia with the UN, arguing that after the collapse of the League of Nations, the mandate for Namibia had ended. Since the General Assembly was unable to influence South Africa's position, it decided to ask the International Court of Justice for an Advisory Opinion. In 1950, the Court found that the mandate for Namibia was still in force and that the UN General Assembly was entitled to supervise South Africa's administration. However, the Court also held that South Africa did not have a legal duty to accept the trusteeship regime.

South Africa did not accept the Court's Advisory Opinion and refused not only to enter into a trusteeship agreement with the UN, but also to accept supervision over the administration of the mandate. Throughout the '50s the General Assembly tried by every possible means to persuade South Africa to change its position. But South Africa, with the support of other colonial countries, refused to comply.

Advisory Opinions of the International Court of Justice are authoritative statements of the law, but they are not binding; only its judgements are binding. For this reason, in 1960 two UN members (Ethiopia and Liberia), which had also been members of the League of Nations, brought an action against South Africa. In 1962, the /contd. p.68

BRITAIN AND NAMIBIA — MAIN HISTORICAL MILESTONES

1795   Britain takes over administration of the Cape Colony from the Dutch. Namibia, as yet, uncolonised.

1866   Cape Colony, still under British control, annexes islands off Namibia's southern coast.

1878   Britain annexes Walvis Bay (Namibia's only deep water port).

1884 — 85   Berlin Conference — Africa is carved up and distributed amongst the European powers. Germany's right to occupy Namibia is confirmed by the Conference states, including Britain.

1915   Following the outbreak of the First World War, Britain requests South Africa to invade Namibia and recover the territory from German rule.

1920   The League of Nations puts Namibia under a trusteeship mandate *"conferred upon His Britannic Majesty to be exercised on his behalf by the Government of the Union of South Africa"*.

1960   The UN General Assembly passes its seminal *"Declaration on the Granting of Independence to Colonial Countries and Peoples"* (UNGA Resolution 1514 (XV), which declares that, *"Colonisation is a denial of fundamental human rights, contrary to the Charter of the United Nations and an impediment to the promotion of world peace; that all peoples have a right to self determination and by virtue of that right they should freely determine their political status and freely pursue their economic, social and cultural development; that inadequacy of political, economic, social and educational preparedness should never serve as a pretext for delaying independence and that all armed action and other repressive measures taken against dependent peoples shall cease; that any attempt aimed at disruption of national unity and territorial integrity is incompatible with the purposes and principles of the UN"*. **Britain abstained in the voting.**

1966   The UN General Assembly terminates South Africa's mandate ordering South Africa to withdraw from Namibia (UNGA Resolution 2145 (XXI)). **Britain abstained in the voting.**

1967   The UN General Assembly establishes the United Nations Council for Namibia (UNCN) to administer Namibia on the UN's behalf until independence (UNGA

Resolution 2248). **Britain abstained in the voting, and does not recognise the UNCN as the legal administering authority for Namibia.**

1971 International Court of Justice gives Advisory Opinion that South Africa occupies Namibia illegally; that the 1966 UNGA Resolution has validly terminated South Africa's mandate; that UN member states have an obligation to recognise the illegality of South Africa's occupation and are to refrain from any dealings with South Africa which imply recognition of its presence in Namibia; that member states are obliged to comply with Security Council (SC) decisions even if they have voted against them; and that South Africa remains accountable for any violations of the rights of the Namibian people. **Britain took the view that in this case it was not bound by relevant SC resolutions, and while acknowledging the illegality of South Africa's occupation, it was nonetheless free to accept that de facto** South Africa was the administering authority, and therefore free to permit continued economic activities of British companies in Namibia.

1974 The UNCN establishes Decree no. 1 for the Protection of Namibia's Natural Resources. **Britain refuses to acknowledge it as binding and therefore under British domestic law, British companies may act in defiance of it**. (NB Britain abstained in the voting in 1967 when the UNGA established the UNCN).

1977 The Contact Group forms to negotiate terms for an independence settlement with South Africa, Britain is a member.

1978 As a Contact Group member, Britain is instrumental in formulating the important SC Resolution 435 outlining terms for a full and early independence.

1978 onwards The Contact Group's efforts fail to secure Namibia's independence due to South African intransigence, which is later compounded by the United States' 'linkage' policy. Britain takes a passive role in the Contact Group, allowing US policies to dominate. Britain consistently refuses to accept calls for mandatory economic sanctions against South Africa, and then agrees to very limited sanctions as part of the October 1985 Commonwealth Accord. The Contact Group fades to inaction, leaving international negotiations in disarray.

International Court of Justice decided that it had jurisdiction to hear the case. But in 1966, in a surprising judgement, the Court reopened the question of jurisdiction and decided that Ethiopia and Liberia did not have standing to sue.

The UN General Assembly reacted by terminating South Africa's mandate (UNGA Res. 2145 (XXI)). It ordered South Africa to withdraw from Namibia, and stated that Namibia was now under the direct responsibility of the UN (Britain abstained in the voting). South Africa, with British support, argued that the UN had no right to terminate the mandate and continued to impose apartheid policies in Namibia.

In 1971, the International Court of Justice responded to the UN Security Council's request for clarification of the implication for member states of South Africa's continued occupation of Namibia. The Court gave an Advisory Opinion that the General Assembly had validly terminated South Africa's mandate and that South Africa's continued occupation was therefore illegal. Furthermore, the Court held that UN member states had an obligation to recognise the illegality of South Africa's occupation and must refrain from any dealings with South Africa implying recognition of a legal South African presence in Namibia.

The Court also held that member states are obliged to comply with Security Council decisions, including those they had voted against; and that South Africa remains accountable for any violations of the rights of Namibians. However, because Advisory Opinions are not binding, South Africa and other states with economic interests in Namibia rejected the Court's opinion.

South Africa and some permanent members of the Security Council (notably Britain) take the view that Security Council resolutions on Namibia are not binding. According to them, only resolutions adopted under Chapter VII of the UN Charter in the case of a breach of peace are binding on member states. The rest are mere recommendations.

The UK position on the 1971 Advisory Opinion is contained in a 'further statement' made in December 1974 by James Callaghan, the then Secretary of State for Foreign and Commonwealth Affairs. Of the Court's findings, he said: *"In October 1971, the Government of the day informed Parliament and the Security Council that it did not accept these conclusions . . ..*

". . . The Government believes that the course of events in the Security Council and the consultations amongst its members do not support the conclusions of fact asserted in the Court's Opinion. And, as a matter of law, they remain of the view that the Security Council cannot take decisions generally binding on member states unless there has been a determination under Article 39 of the existence of a threat to the peace, a breach of the peace or an act of aggression. Consequently, they are unable to accept this part of the Advisory Opinion.

"However, for the reasons explained above, the Government takes the view that South Africa is in occupation without title of a territory which

has international status. This occupation is unlawful and South Africa should withdraw. Meanwhile, South Africa remains the de facto Administering Authority. However, in the circumstances, there is an obligation on states not to recognise any right of South Africa to continue to administer the Territory. But there is no obligation, in the absence of appropriate decisions under Chapter VII of the Charter, to take measures which are in the nature of sanctions. It follows that we do not accept an obligation to take active measures of pressure to limit or stop commercial or industrial relations of our nationals with the South African administration of Namibia." [3]

According to the restrictive interpretation of the powers of the Security Council followed by the British Government and other permanent members of the Security Council, member states are under no obligation to break economic links with Namibia unless a sanctions resolution is adopted. Since, according to the UN Charter, such a resolution can only be adopted if **all** permanent members of the Security Council agree, the possibility of taking action against South Africa can be blocked by any one of the five permanent members. That is, the UK, the USA, France, the USSR and China can each paralyse the Security Council by vetoing draft resolutions which call for sanctions against South Africa.

Thus there is an enormous gap between the well-established international legal consensus on Namibia and reality. The consensus is that South Africa's presence in Namibia is illegal. Furthermore, it is agreed that the struggle of Namibia's people against the occupying power is a legitimate exercise of the right of self-determination, and the UN is acknowledged to have direct responsibility for the administration of the territory.

But the voting record shows that permanent member states of the Security Council, Britain among them, have used an array of technical arguments to justify their failure to act in accordance with United Nations decisions. A new statement of international political will, followed by appropriate action, is now vital to bring about an early realisation of the Namibian people's rights to self-determination and independence. [4]

Protecting Namibia's natural resources

In 1967 the General Assembly established the United Nations Council for Namibia (UNCN); Britain abstained. The UNCN's role is to administer Namibia on the UN's behalf until independence. The first full-time UN Commissioner for Namibia was appointed in early 1974 to work through the UNCN with the goal of asserting the Council's administrative mandate over Namibia. In October 1974, the UNCN established its **Decree for the Protection of the Natural Resources of Namibia** — Decree no. 1 — (see Appendix 2 for full text). It was a bid to discourage the economic exploitation of Namibia's natural resources by South Africa and its main western trading partners, notably the UK.

Under the terms of Decree no. 1 the UN became entitled to seize any exports leaving Namibia without the written permission of the UNCN, and any *"person, entity or corporation"* contravening the Decree may be held liable for damages by the future government of an independent Namibia.

The British Government does not recognise Decree no. 1 on the grounds that the UN General Assembly acted beyond its competence in establishing the UNCN. The British Government does not recognise the UNCN as the legal administering authority for Namibia and therefore does not accept UNCN decisions as binding.[5]

Consequently, the Decree has had little impact on Britain's trading links with Namibia. As the Chairman of one the main British companies operating in Namibia, the Rio Tinto Zinc Corporation,[6] stated: *"As a company we are subject to the laws of the countries in which we operate, and particularly as a British company to those of the UK. United Nations resolutions do not apply to a company unless they are made part of the laws of a jurisdiction to which the company is subject. This has not happened in the UK so far as the relevant United Nations resolutions are concerned. Successive British administrations have refused to accept their validity, and in detailing their reasons for this in a number of ministerial statements over the years, have made it clear that our activities in relation to Rössing are not illegal."* [7]

ECONOMIC LINKS

British economic links with Namibia are considerable. In 1985 forty-five British companies operated there, in a variety of sectors including mining, banking, petroleum and insurance (see Appendix 3 for list of UK companies). Other Contact Group states have far fewer companies operating in Namibia. According to a United Nations report the USA has 24 companies, West Germany has 4, Canada has 4, and France has 3.[8]

Accurate figures for overall foreign investment in Namibia are difficult to ascertain. Namibia belongs to the Rand Monetary Area (South Africa, Lesotho, Swaziland and Namibia) and as such is an integral part of South Africa for the purpose of tariffs, trade and exchange control regulations. This means that separate trade and investment flow figures for Namibia are not normally published.

Amongst the largest British companies operating in Namibia are Rio Tinto Zinc (RTZ) and Barclays Bank (through its South African associate Barclays National). RTZ has a major holding in Rössing Uranium Ltd, which operates an open-pit mine and processing plant producing uranium oxide near Swakopmund in western Namibia. Rössing Uranium Ltd provided RTZ with £7.3 million net attributable profit in 1984 and £14.6 million in 1983 (the large difference being due mainly to the fact that the South African administration allowed Rössing to defer tax payments until it had recovered its capital costs, and also due to the weakened rand when translated into sterling).[9]

Barclays National is the largest commercial bank operating in Namibia with an estimated 50% of the R714 million (£423 million) of total bank deposits in Namibia at the end of 1983.[10]

The economic involvement of British companies in Namibia adds to Britain's responsibility for the existing situation. British companies in Namibia pay taxes to the South African-controlled administration in

The economic involvement of British companies in Namibia adds to Britain's responsibilities for the existing situation.

71

Windhoek and must be licensed by either the South African Government or the South African administration in Namibia. Thus they tacitly support South Africa's illegal occupation of Namibia and their tax payments directly contribute to equipping, deploying and maintaining the SWATF, the South African-controlled military forces in Namibia. In the year 1981 — 82, Barclays National is reported to have paid R750,000 (£425,000) to the Windhoek administration in tax on its profits made in Namibia. Rössing Uranium Ltd. is estimated to have paid R30 million (£17.78 million) in tax on its operations in 1983, and a similar amount in 1984.[11]

Those British companies operating in Namibia which are involved in exploiting and depleting its natural resources do so in defiance of the UNCN's Decree no. 1 which aims to protect these resources for the benefit of Namibia's people. In contrast to independent resource-rich countries which have either nationalised the extractive industries, or imposed taxes and other measures to obtain a fair share of the benefits derived, in Namibia's case the bulk of profits earned by transnational companies are regularly exported.

British companies operating in Namibia also benefit from low taxation. Since the majority of Namibians have no say in how taxes are fixed or spent, they suffer the effects of desperately inadequate public health, education and other services. Foreign economic interests are contributing to economic growth at the expense of national development based on meeting the needs of the poor majority.

There is no obligation on British (or other foreign) companies operating in Namibia to create educational and training opportunities for black Namibians over and above the training necessary for the companies' own operations. Enlightened self-interest has, for example, led RTZ to fund the Rössing Foundation's training programme for blacks in Namibia. But schemes of this kind are not enough, given the enormous inequalities in educational opportunity and the overriding need to tackle the causes of this inequality.

Such labour legislation as exists has been enacted more in the interests of the colonial economy than of the labour force. Working conditions and the type of provision made for housing are effectively left to the discretion of individual companies. Even the voluntary EEC Code of Conduct, established to promote minimum conditions for workers employed by European companies operating in South Africa, could not legitimately extend into Namibia because of the illegal status of South Africa's occupation. In any event, it would be no substitute for enlightened labour legislation enacted by a democratically elected national government.

Poverty, the high rate of unemployment, the near total lack of black Trade Unions and the repressive labour legislation all militate against the bargaining power of blacks in the labour market. Moreover, British companies in Namibia are not accountable to any authority — either in Namibia itself or here in Europe — which represents the interests of black workers.

BRITISH AID TO NAMIBIA

Britain's bilateral aid programme to Namibia began in 1978, the year when SC Resolution 435 was negotiated by the Contact Group. Unlike other bilateral aid commitments it is not administered on a government to government basis. In 1984/85, British aid to Namibia totalled £474,000 — just over a fifteenth of RTZ's net attributable profits from Rössing Uranium for the same year.[12] Britain's aid to Namibia 1985/86 is estimated to be £700,000.[13]

The British aid programme includes the costs of three long-term English language teaching appointments to the United Nations Institute for Namibia in Lusaka, one teaching post at the Namibian Extension Unit in Lusaka and 50 awards for Namibian students, mainly in English language teaching and public administration. It also covers a Books Presentation Programme for educational work inside Namibia, as well as for Namibian refugees in Angola and Zambia and a discretionary fund for supporting **non-governmental** development and welfare projects inside Namibia, administered by the British Embassy in Pretoria.[14]

In addition to bilateral aid, awards are made under Britain's multilateral aid programme to the United Nations Educational Training Programme for Southern Africa (UNETPSA) which was awarded £500,000 in 1983. Some Namibians are among the beneficiaries of UNETPSA's work.[15]

In Oxfam's view, it is important that Britain and other aid donors continue their policy of not giving aid to the illegal administration in Namibia and that no aid is used indirectly to support South African-controlled structures and institutions. Thus the need for international assistance to Namibia's people is a compelling argument for full and early independence.

The irony of the present situation is that British companies are free to profit from Namibian resources, whilst the British Government is not free to assist Namibia's people.

BRITAIN'S LINKS WITH SOUTH AFRICA

It is not the purpose of this book to trace the complex web of historical, social, economic, political, and strategic relationships which Britain has with South Africa. However, it is important to note that Britain has extensive connections with South Africa, and that successive British governments have been primarily protecting British interests in South Africa in evading action under international law to bring independence to Namibia.

INTERNATIONAL ECONOMIC MEASURES

As international pressure to institute economic sanctions against South Africa mounts, it is important to identify the key issues relating to Namibia as these are often confused with the parallel debate concerning sanctions as a means to abolish apartheid in South Africa.

Firstly, there is the question of sanctions against South Africa on the grounds that these would speed up its withdrawal from Namibia, preparing the way for implementation of Resolution 435. And secondly, there is the question of the legality of foreign companies operating in Namibia.

On the question of sanctions against South Africa, as far as the role of the UN is concerned, Britain holds the view that Security Council Resolutions are not binding on member states, and that only resolutions adopted under Chapter VII of the UN Charter are binding. This view runs counter to the Advisory Opinion of the International Court of Justice. Moreover Britain, as a permanent member of the Security Council, is in a position to veto the adoption of any resolution calling for sanctions against South Africa under Chapter VII. Thus according to its restrictive interpretation of the powers of the Security Council, Britain is not bound to break economic links with South Africa because of its illegal occupation of Namibia.

However, in other international fora, Britain is less able to deflect pressure for sanctions. For example, Britain's hitherto anti-sanctions position has been slightly modified by pressure from other Commonwealth states. The Commonwealth communiqué issued in October 1985 was specifically critical of South Africa's illegal occupation. It stated: *Heads of Government were gravely concerned that Namibia's independence had been further delayed . . . (and) recalled that in New Delhi they had agreed that if South Africa continued to obstruct the implementation of Resolution 435, the adoption of appropriate measures under the Charter of the United Nations would have to be considered."* [16] The communiqué also stated that the goal of *"ensuring South Africa's compliance with the wishes of the international community on the question of Namibia"* was an important reason for the Commonwealth agreement to impose limited sanctions against South Africa, with the possibility of imposing more stringent sanctions later.

On the second question of the legality in international law of foreign economic interests in Namibia, the principal statement is the International Court of Justice's Advisory Opinion of 1971. This stated that: *"The restraints which are implicit in the non-recognition of South Africa's presence in Namibia . . . impose upon member states the obligation to abstain from entering into economic and other forms of relationship or dealings with South Africa on behalf of or concerning Namibia which may entrench its authority over the Territory."*

Since all foreign companies operating in Namibia do so with some form of permission, concession or licence either from the South African Government or from the South African-controlled administration in Namibia, they are clearly acting contrary to the spirit of the ICJ Advisory Opinion.

However, successive British governments have refused to accept the Court's findings unless the UN adopts a resolution calling for sanctions under Chapter VII of the UN Charter.[17] The irony of the situation is that Britain can use its veto in the Security Council to block such a resolution, whilst in theory remaining in favour of UN efforts to achieve Namibian independence. The British Foreign and Commonwealth Office recently stated: *"In keeping with the spirit of various United Nations resolutions, we give no promotional support to any form of trade with Namibia . . . However, there are no mandatory resolutions prohibiting trade with the territory and it is, therefore, our view that this is a matter for commercial decision only."* [18]

Further, on the grounds that the UN General Assembly acted beyond its competence in establishing the United Nations Council for Namibia (UNCN), successive British governments have not recognised the UNCN's Decree no. 1 for the Protection of the Natural Resources of Namibia. Thus, the provisions of Decree no. 1 have not been incorporated into British domestic law to prevent British nationals and companies from operating in or trading with Namibia. While this remains the case, British companies continue to operate in Namibia in defiance of international law, maintaining they are doing nothing **illegal**.

Having identified the two principal issues concerning international economic measures with respect to Namibia, a brief summary is necessary of the main arguments for and against sanctions as a legitimate form of pressure in order to outline the framework in which Oxfam's Namibian partners make their statements.

THE INVOLVEMENT OF FOREIGN COMPANIES IN NAMIBIA AND SOUTH AFRICA

Different viewpoints exist on the role of foreign economic interests in Namibia and South Africa, and consequently on action that should be taken regarding foreign investments as part of the international effort to secure Namibia's independence. The different views can be broadly categorised as follows: firstly, there are those who believe that the role of companies and investments is simply to generate profits for their shareholders. According to this argument, companies do not have a political role to play and should be free to operate in all political environments, Namibia and South Africa included.

The second broad category of opinion is that foreign companies, through their economic activities, can be a force for evolutionary political change, particularly if they adopt 'enlightened' employment and other social policies and also if they form relationships with the governments of the countries in which they operate, with a view to promoting internal political reforms. Barclays PLC, for example, states: *"Barclays National Bank operates on a commercial basis and the successful growth of our associate, together with its long-standing liberalising policies, is a force for justice in helping to improve the lot of the underprivileged people in South Africa and Namibia"*. [19]

The third viewpoint holds that foreign companies, by virtue of their economic involvement in Namibia and South Africa, necessarily buttress the political interests of the host government and their presence is therefore an integral part of the prevailing political system for as long as they remain in the country. This argument maintains that only by terminating, or at least severely limiting, their activities would pressure for change be effected.

The economic dimension of the first two approaches is that the activities of foreign companies eventually benefit the black majority in South Africa and Namibia, by creating wealth, jobs and skills and thus effectively a gradual 'trickledown' improvement in living standards. The argument goes that because they contribute to the creation of wealth in the country, it therefore follows that their withdrawal would hurt the economy and, in turn, the living standards and employment opportunities of black Namibians and South Africans.

The economic dimensions of the arguments from those who oppose foreign investment are that foreign companies operating in Namibia and South Africa do so in an environment where the extreme inequalities of wealth between whites and blacks are morally indefensible. They hold that the majority of Namibian and South African blacks, those who live in the 'homelands', are among the poorest people in Africa and that the 'trickledown' argument is therefore meaningless. They also argue that foreign companies operating in South Africa and Namibia, regardless of whether they offer improved working conditions or fund social welfare projects, have nonetheless to operate within the unjust legal framework of the host country. Moreover the debilitating social consequences of South Africa's illegal occupation, such as divided families, inadequate schooling and health care, loss of dignity, deprivation of citizenship and the right to vote, are not addressed by the economic arguments put forward in favour of foreign investment.

The political dimensions of the views put forward in favour of continued foreign investment are that economic sanctions would only serve to harden the South African Government's line. It is argued that sanctions have been shown not to work. In the case of Rhodesia, for example, it is held that international economic sanctions, far from crippling the economy, made it more robust by promoting self-sufficiency. The view is expressed that for as long as foreign companies remain in Namibia and South Africa they can promote constructive political change by being critical of government at the same time as giving practical examples of improved living and working conditions — if they withdrew they would be powerless to exert this pressure.

There is also the view that because the South African economy provides jobs for thousands of migrant workers from neighbouring

African countries, disinvestment and sanctions would harm the interests of other countries which derive benefit from those workers' remittances. This, it is argued, should be set against the possible benefits of sanctions.

The political dimensions of opposition to foreign investment are that since all efforts on the part of foreign investors have so far failed to secure either Namibia's independence or the abolition of apartheid, it is time to apply different, stronger measures such as economic sanctions.

On this point, a statement issued by the Commonwealth Conference in October 1985, held that, *"We are united in the belief that reliance on the range of pressures adopted so far has not resulted in the fundamental changes we have sought over many years . . . We consider that the situation calls for urgent practical steps."* [20]

It is maintained that international sanctions would be an effective tool to achieve change in Namibia and South Africa because the two economies are so strongly integrated with foreign interests. Economic sanctions are also widely seen as a means of applying peaceful pressure for change. It is argued that the majority of black Namibians and South Africans would rather undergo the economic hardships caused by sanctions now than continue to endure escalating violence and the economic, political and social deprivations they suffer at present.

With regard to the argument that workers from neighbouring African states would be hurt by sanctions, the case is put that for as long as apartheid rule continues in South Africa, neighbouring African countries will continue to suffer from South Africa's regional policy of economic, political and military destabilisation and that the removal of apartheid will be in the long-term interests of these countries. It is also pointed out that the Southern African 'Frontline States' have themselves repeatedly called for sanctions against South Africa. President Kenneth Kaunda of Zambia, for example, at a joint meeting of foreign ministers of the Frontline States and the EEC in February 1986 stated: *"We have been informed that the European Communities stand for peaceful change. That is also our stand. It is for this reason that we have advocated economic sanctions against South Africa because we believe that these measures are a peaceful means of bringing about the desired change in that country.*

"We are quite aware of the effects such measures will have on both the black people in South Africa and on the economies of the Frontline States. There is no denying the fact that the majority of Frontline States are dependent on South Africa for the survival of their economies. In spite of this, we are prepared to suffer a little now rather than much more later when the racial volcano in South Africa eventually erupts. Its lava will spread to all corners of this region, killing and maiming many people in its trail; for there is no way in which this tragedy can be avoided if South Africa does not take the measures we have advocated and continue to advocate." [21]

THE VIEWS OF OXFAM'S PARTNERS IN NAMIBIA

The interminable delays over independence, and the century-long struggle against poverty and oppression have combined to produce a mounting frustration amongst black Namibians, many of whom feel that decisive action from the international community is urgently needed.

Mass rally in June 1985 protesting against the official inauguration of the South African-controlled interim government.

The views of Oxfam's major partners in Namibia are admirably summed up in the following statement by the Evangelical Lutheran Ovambo-Kavango Church (ELOC):

"The dispute over Namibia has gone on for almost twenty years. Those twenty years, added to the eighty-two years of colonisation, makes it over one hundred years during which many lives of innocent citizens have been lost, and much of the wealth of the land plundered.

"This situation is still continuing . . . The Church is thus forced to declare its position on the issue of sanctions against the South African Government. And in this . . . the Church is a spokesman for the people of this country.

"The Church does not take its position with a blind eye, without anticipating any new suffering which may accompany the implementation of sanctions. New suffering may befall both the whites and blacks. But the Church is convinced that those suffering are the only alternative to avoid the shedding of blood.

"The voice emanating from the muzzle of the gun is not favoured by the Church. The peaceful negotiations that were undertaken in the past were ineffective. Now, only one avenue remains open: to isolate South Africa by all means.

"It is clear that the Church is not advocating isolation of South Africa out of hatred . . . The Church is doing it in good faith, so that all those who have a say in the affairs of this country, through negotiations, will give the whole nation the right to choose its desired and true leaders." [22]

As one old man in an impoverished southern 'homeland' said,

"I am tired of all the talking about Namibian independence. The only thing that I see is that the western powers must take sides. If they support South Africa, they must say so. If they are on our side, then they must take action against South Africa. Someone who hasn't suffered oppression cannot know what it is — western countries don't understand how we feel." [24]

SUMMARY AND KEY CONSIDERATIONS

"As mothers, we are really concerned about our children's future. We want to send a message straight to the British Government: he should use his power and pressure so that we can get back our country." (Woman farmer, southern Namibia.[1])

South Africa's continued illegal occupation of Namibia means that the majority of Namibia's people live in conditions of great poverty and deprivation, in spite of the fact that Namibia is among Africa's wealthiest countries. It also means that black Namibians have no basic rights, and are subject to a wide range of repressive legislation.

The South African-controlled economy is geared towards the interests of foreign investors and settlers and keeps the black majority in poverty.

Namibian resources are exploited by foreign interests in defiance of international law, and precious natural resources are being depleted with minimal benefit to the poor majority.

Social development for the black majority is severely hindered by the present colonial structures. Basic services for blacks are disgracefully inadequate and the lack of decent educational facilities has resulted in an acute shortage of skilled black Namibians. The war causes widespread misery, death and destruction. Only a just political settlement will bring it to an end, although even after independence huge obstacles to tackling poverty and underdevelopment will remain.

International efforts to help Namibia achieve independence under majority rule have foundered over the conflicting interests of powerful states. Meanwhile, Namibia's people continue to suffer under South African occupation, denied the right to govern their country and to shape their own society.

Historically, politically and economically, Britain has been closely connected with Namibia for well over a century, and consequently carries a heavy responsibility to help it achieve independence.

The following key considerations are based on Oxfam's experience of more than 20 years' work in Namibia.

1: A fresh initiative for unconditional independence

The overwhelming need to achieve full and early independence for Namibia, according to the United Nations Security Council Resolution 435, is more urgent than ever before.

The extreme poverty and denial of basic human needs are Oxfam's particular concerns. Until Namibians can run their own country under an elected government, they cannot begin to address these pressing problems.

Britain should recognise its important historical role and take a fresh and urgent initiative to press for Namibia's unconditional independence in accordance with SC Resolution 435, and should avoid the 'linkage' precondition in current US-led negotiations.

2: Recognition of Decree no. 1

Meanwhile, the British Government should take steps to ensure that British-based companies operating in Namibia do not take advantage of the Namibian people's powerlessness to control their country's economy and natural resources.

Until Namibia is independent, the activities of British-based companies operating in Namibia are contrary to the spirit of international law, and are morally highly questionable in the light of the extreme poverty perpetuated by present economic and political structures.

The British Government should formally recognise the United Nations Council for Namibia's Decree no. 1 for the Protection of the Natural Resources of Namibia and act on its provisions.

3: The views of Oxfam's partners in Namibia

The British Government should give careful consideration to the views expressed by Oxfam's partners in Namibia on the question of economic sanctions against South Africa as a means to speed up implementation of Security Council Resolution 435.

4: Aid

On independence, British and EEC official aid to Namibia should be generous in scale and fully in accordance with the needs of the majority.

In the meantime the British Government should ensure that sufficient bilateral and multilateral humanitarian aid is allocated to Namibian refugees.

Notes and References

General Notes

Racial terminology. The South African Government uses the general term 'blacks' or 'Africans' to denote all the indigenous 'population groups' (as classified by the South African authorities) except for 'coloureds' which is a South African term denoting people of mixed race ancestry. In this book, 'blacks' is used as a common term for all non-white Namibians except where, in order to explain apartheid in action, we have used single inverted commas to distinguish between 'blacks' and 'coloureds' in the South African sense.

Currency Conversions. The South African rand is the unit of currency used in Namibia. All figures expressed in rand have been converted into sterling, except for GDP and GNP figures which are given in $US. Where a year-average figure is used, we have followed the IMF (International Monetary Fund) year-average conversion rates. Otherwise, the prevailing *Financial Times* conversion rates are used.

In order to protect the Namibians who have been quoted throughout the book, we have either used no names at all or have used first names only.

Namibia – Basic Facts

1   Includes Walvis Bay and Namibian refugees, exludes non-local military personnel. Projections based on Green R.H., Kiljunen M., Kiljunen K., *Namibia the Last Colony*, 1981, p. 260; and SWA/Namibia Directorate of Development Co-ordination, *National Atlas of South West Africa*, 1983.
2   Estimates based on Moorsom R., *Transforming a Wasted Land*, A Future for Namibia series, No. 2, CIIR, 1982, p. 99; and Green R.K., Kiljunen M. & K., op. cit., p. 262.
3   Estimates based on SWA/Namibia , Dept. of Finance, *Statistical/Economic Review*, SWA/Namibia Information Services, 1984; and SWA/Namibia, Directorate of Development Co-ordination, op. cit.
4   Gross income for whites includes salaries and local business profits but excludes corporate surpluses; for blacks includes wages, profits and subsistence output. (Sources as in footnote 3 above, and projections based on Green R.H., Kiljunen M. & K., op. cit.)
5   UNIN, *Health Sector Policy Options for Independent Namibia*, 1984, p. 19.
6   Ellis J., *Education, Repression and Liberation: Namibia*, A Future for Namibia series, No. 4, CIIR, 1984, p. 70.
7   CIIR, *Profile Namibia*, 1985
8   Ellis J., op. cit., p. 41.

Chronology

1 Sources: IDOC International, *Namibia: The Strength of the Powerless*, 1980, pp. v — xix.
   SWAPO Department of Information & Publicity, *To Be Born a Nation; the Liberation Struggle for Namibia*, 1981, pp. 301 — 310.
   CIIR, *Profile on Namibia*, 1985.
   Racism and Apartheid in Southern Africa: South Africa and Namibia, UNESCO Press, Paris, 1974.
   The Guardian, 5.3.1986.

Introduction

1 UNIN, op. cit., p. 19.
2 UNCN, *The Military Situation in and Relating to Namibia, Report of Standing Committee II of the UNCN*, 1984, p. 3.
   SWAPO (South West Africa People's Organisation) was founded in 1960 and leads the national liberation movement of Namibia. It is not banned inside Namibia, but operates under constant harassment and repression by the security forces. SWAPO organises large refugee settlements in Angola and Zambia.
3 Ibid.
4 Fraenkel P., Murray R., *The Namibians*, Minority Rights Group, 1985, p. 5.
5 Text, Mandate for South West Africa, Article 2.
6 SWAPO Department of Information and Publicity, *To Be Born a Nation: the Liberation Struggle for Namibia*, 1981, p. 123.
7 Hanlon, J., *Beggar Your Neighbour: Apartheid Power in Southern Africa*, CIIR and James Currie, 1986.
8 *Hansard*, 23.1.85.

Oxfam's Namibia Programme

1 *Grants to Namibian Refugees: May 1985 — Feb. 1986*

World University Service	— Training for Kindergarten teachers	£ 1,301
	— Books for refugee camp workers	26
Namibia Support Committee	— Medical Kits, Angola	14,896
	— Journals for SWAPO medical staff	449
Namibia Extension Unit, Lusaka	— Coordinator's salary	2,830

2 Personal interview with author, Katatura, September, 1985.
3 Personal interview with author, Windhoek, October, 1985.

Chapter 1

1 Estimates based on SWA/Namibia Dept. of Finance, *Statistical/Economic Review 1984*, SWA/Namibia Information Service, Windhoek; and SWA/Namibia Directorate of Development Coordination, *National Atlas of South West Africa, 1983*; and projections based on Green R. H., Kiljunen M., Kiljunen K., *Namibia The Last Colony*, 1981.
2 Ibid.
3 An estimated 50-55% (1983) of GDP is exported. Estimate based on SWA/Namibia Dept. of Finance, op. cit.

4 1983 figures give the following GDP distribution figures; gross profits for transnational corporations and local businesses R820m (40% of GDP), taxes R410m (20%), salaries to whites R370m (18%), income left over for all blacks R450m (22%), income to black workers R300m (14%), to black traders and business people R45m (2%), to black peasant farmers R105m (6%).
See note (1) above for sources.

5 Estimate based on SWA/Namibia, Dept. of Finance, op. cit.

6 Personal interview with author, Katatura, Sept. 1985.

7 Following the International Court of Justice's 1966 Judgement which held that Ethiopia and Liberia did not have standing to bring an action against South Africa (see section on International Law, Chapter 3).

8 The Development of Self-Government for Native Nations in South West Africa Act of 1968 (No. 54) implemented the 'native affairs' part of the 'homelands' programme, and the South West African Affairs Act of 1969 (No. 25) transferred administrative functions from the then white Legislative Assembly in Namibia to the South African Parliament and State President so that South Africa had direct control of the 'homelands' programme.

9 IDAF, *Namibia the Facts*, 1980, p. 15.

10 The Development of Self-Government for Native Nations Amendment Act of 1978 (No. 20), IDAF, 1980, op. cit., p. 15 & 16.

11 Ibid, p. 64.

12 Ibid, p. 17.

13 Ibid, pp. 27 & 28.

14 Ibid, p. 28.

15 IDAF, Focus no. 2, July 1981.

16 Personal Interview with author, central Namibia, Sept. 1985.

17 IDAF, Focus No. 63, March/April 1986.

18 Personal interview with author, central Namibia, Sept. 1985.

19 Personal interview with author, Katatura, Sept. 1985.

20 Personal interview with author, Katatura, Sept 1985.

21 Personal interview with author, central Namibia, Sept. 1985.

22 Personal interview with author, Katatura, Sept. 1985.

23 Potgieter J.F., *The Household Subsistence Level of the Major Urban Centres of the Republic of South Africa*, University of Port Elizabeth Institute for Planning Research, Sept. 1983.

24 Personal communication with author, Windhoek, September, 1985.

25 Abrahams O., "Namibia Today: The Internal Situation", article published in *The Namibia Review*, no. 28, April — June 1983.

26 Personal interview with author, central Namibia, Sept. 1985.

27 Moorsom R., *Transforming a Wasted Land*, A Future for Namibia Series, No.2, CIIR, 1982, p. 21.

28 Derived from Moorsom, 1982, op. cit, p. 99. Also Green R. H. & Kiljunen M. & K. op. cit, p. 262.

29 Adapted from SWAPO Dept. of Information and Publicity, *To Be Born a Nation - The Liberation Struggle for Namibia*, 1983, p. 62.

30 In 1983, 290,000 people (50% of the economically active population, using this category to mean people over 12 years not in school available for employment, rather than those in employment) relied for their main subsistence on peasant agriculture; 45,000 people (8%) were employed on white-owned farms including domestic servants and proprietors. Estimates based on Green R. H., Kiljunen M. & K., op. cit, p. 264.

31 Moorsom R., op. cit, p. 37.

32 UNCN, *Activities of Foreign Economic Interests Operating in Namibia*, Report of Standing Committee II of the UNCN, 1984, p. 16.

33 Ibid, p. 2. Estimate of % GDP based on SWA/Namibia, Dept. of Finance op. cit, and projection based on Green R. H. & Kiljunen M. & K., op. cit, pp. 276 & 285. This figure is lower than in previous years because of the drought. According to Green et

al, in 1979 the commercial agricultural sector accounted for 9.8% of GDP. % of exports based on SWA/Namibia Dept. of Finance, op. cit.

34 Green R. H., Kiljunen M. & K., op. cit. p. 38.

35 Moorsom R., The Plunder Continues, *Action on Namibia* bulletin, NSC, 1982.

36 Park, P. and Jackson, T., *Lands of Plenty, Lands of Scarcity: Agricultural Policy and Peasant Farmers in Zimbabwe and Tanzania*, Oxfam, 1985, pp. 3-10.

37 One recent estimate gives R35,000 per ranch per year over the drought period as the average subsidy. Source CIIR report, 1985, p. 5.

38 Ibid, p. 5.

39 In practice many white farm owners leave the day-to-day management of their farms to black employees, often for long periods at a time. There is, therefore, some considerable management expertise amongst blacks (although few are given adequate recognition for the responsibility they carry), which will be indispensable for post-independence manpower requirements.

40 Personal interview with author, central Namibia, Sept. 1985.

41 Based on Moorsom R., *Transforming a Wasted Land*, A Future for Namibia series, No. 2, CIIR, 1982, p. 96.

42 It is important, in general, to avoid use of the term 'subsistence' when referring to black agricultural production as the resource base available to peasant farming households is inadequate to support them at subsistence level.

43 Moorsom R., op. cit, p. 9.

44 Fraenkel P., Murray R., *The Namibians*, Minority Rights Group report no. 19, 1985, p. 20.

45 Oxfam internal memorandum, Jan. 1986.

46 Fraenkel P., Murray R., op. cit, p. 26.

47 Personal interview with author, central Namibia, Sept. 1985.

48 Personal interview with author, central Namibia, Sept. 1985.

49 The transnational corporations from the Contact Group states, which operate or invest in Namibia, either directly or through associate companies, include: *UK* — Rio Tinto Zinc Corporation PLC (RTZ), Consolidated Goldfields PLC, Selection Trust Ltd.; *USA* — Newport Mining Corporation; *Canada* — Rio Algom Ltd.; *France* — Total-Compagnie Miniere et Nucleaire; *West Germany* — Urangesellschaft, mbH. Transnationals are also involved either directly or through associate companies in uranium prospecting operations in Namibia. These are reported to include: *UK* — RTZ (through Rössing Uranium Ltd.); *USA* — Union Carbide Corporation, Newport Mining Corporation; *France* — Societe Nationale Elf Aquitaine (SNEA), Pechiney-Ugine Kuhlmann, Compagnie Francaise des Petroles (CFP), Entreprise de Recherche et d'Activites Petrolieres (ERAP).
Source: UNCN, op. cit, pp. 6, 9, 11, 14.

50 Ibid, pp. 8, 9, 11.

51 CIIR, *Mines and Independence*, A Future for Namibia Series, No. 3, 1983, p. 29.

52 Estimate based on SWA/Namibia, Dept. of Finance, op. cit.

53 CIIR, op. cit, p. 29.

54 Green R. H., Kiljunen M. & K., op. cit,, p. 37.

55 Based on Green R. H., Kiljunen M. & K., op. cit.

56 Fraenkel P., Murray R., op. cit, p. 25.

57 Estimates based on SWA/Namibia, Dept. of Finance, op. cit, and CIIR, op. cit, p. 145.

58 CIIR report, 1985, p. 2.

59 Moorsom R., *Exploiting the Sea*, A Future for Namibia series, No. 5, 1984, p. 16.

60 Ibid, p. 16.

61 UNCN, op. cit, p. 17.

62 Green R. H. Kiljunen M. & K., op. cit, p. 40.

63 Estimate based on Moorsom R., op. cit, pp. 19, 29, 104.

64 Estimate based on Green R. H., Kiljunen M. & K. op cit p. 40; and Moorsom R., op. cit.

65 CIIR report, 1985, p. 6.

66 In 1974 R22m (£13.8m) and 1975 R20m (£12.6m) post tax profits from the inshore industry (including the South African fisheries run by the companies operating Namibia's inshore industry).
Source: Moorsom R., op. cit, p. 111.
67 Ibid p. 57.
68 Ibid, pp. 57, 58.
69 Ibid, p. 58.
70 Ibid, p. 35. Exclusive Economic Zones determine that a coastal state is entitled to extend its control of marine and seabed resources to a distance of 379 km.
71 Ibid, p. 36.
72 Ibid, p. 36.
73 According to Moorsom (Ibid pp. 70-94) however, a state-planned revival of the inshore industry, after independence, would unfortunately involve a reduction in the numbers employed in the short term.

Chapter 2

1 Personal interview with author, Windhoek, October 1985.
2 *The Namibian*, 24.1.86.
3 Personal interview with author, Central Namibia, September 1985.
4 Ellis, J. *Education, Repression and Liberation: Namibia*, A Future for Namibia series, No. 4, CIIR, 1984, pp. 36 & 70.
5 In 1981, an average of R1,210 (£707) was spent on each white pupil, as compared to R232 (£135) for each 'black' pupil, and R300 (£175) for each 'coloured' pupil. Ibid, p. 41.
6 A survey conducted by the United Nations Institute for Namibia in 1979 revealed that 'blacks' had to contribute R20 to R50 (£11 to £27) towards state schooling per child and R80 to R105 (£44 to £58) towards mission schooling.
7 CIIR, *Profile Namibia*, 1982.
8 See Ellis J., op. cit, for a full discussion on the Cape syllabus.
9 Personal interview with author, Oxford, January 1986.
10 UNIN, Towards a Language Policy for Namibia, 1981, p. 7.
11 Ellis J., op. cit, p. 36.
12 According to UNIN's 1985 revised estimates, the commercial agricultural sector will need to fill 1,750 new posts at independence; 3,000 new posts in education will need to be filled; 850 in health; 3,750 in general government; 1,750 in mining; 1,550 in transport and communications; and 300 in fisheries.
13 UNIN, *Manpower Estimates and Development Implications for Namibia*, 1978, p. 12.
14 Personal interview with author, central Namibia, September 1985.
15 Personal interview with author, Ovamboland, October 1985.
16 Personal interview with author, Ovamboland, October 1985.
17 Personal interview with author, Windhoek, October 1985. A pilot government literacy programme is reported to be in progress, but NLP officials say that it is presently very limited in scope, and that it is using Afrikaans in preference to indigenous languages or English.
18 Oxfam internal memorandum, January 1984.
19 Namibia Refugee Project, *Dossier on Literacy in the Namibian Refugee Settlements*, 1985, p. 34.
20 UNGA Resolution 2679 (XXL).
21 UNIN, *Manpower Estimates and Development Implications for Namibia*, 1978 p. v.
22 ODA, Information Brief on Namibia, 1985.
23 The technical use of the term 'infant' means babies under 1 year, and is thus used throughout this section.
24 Infant mortality rate (IMR) statistics are expressed as a given number per 1,000 live births. UNIN estimates the IMR for blacks in Namibia to be 155 using official figures

for 1977-78 (UNIN, *Health Sector Policy Options for Independent Namibia*, 1984, p. 19). IPPF World Population Data Sheet, 1982 gives average IMR for Africa as 121 (based on 1979-80 statistics). It should be noted that average IMR statistics (whether expressed for a national population or, as in this case, for a racial sub-category) mask internal inequalities in health and wealth.

25 Personal interview with author, Ovamboland, October 1985.
26 Personal interview with author, Katatura, September 1985.
27 UNIN, *Health Sector Policy Options for Independent Namibia*, 1984, p. 21.
28 Ibid, p. 20.
29 Ibid, p. 20.
30 NSC Health Collective, *Namibia: Reclaiming the People's Health*, 1984, p. 11.
31 UNIN, op. cit, p. 23.
32 Ibid, p. 25.
33 Ibid, p. 60.
34 Personal interview with author, Katatura, September 1985.
35 Maundjua P. E, *My Impressions of the Life of Women in Katatura*, 1985.
36 Personal interview with author, Katatura, September 1985.
37 NSC Health Collective, op. cit, p. 99.
38 Simon D., "The Crisis in Namibian Health Services", published in the *Namibian Review*, no. 28, April/June 1983, p. 19.
39 NSC Health Collective, op. cit, p. 13.
40 UNIN, op. cit, p. 49.
41 Oxfam internal memorandum, October 1985.
42 Personal interview with author, Ovamboland, October 1985.
43 UNIN, op. cit, p. 52.
44 World Bank, *World Development Report*, 1985.
45 UNIN, op. cit. p. 52.
46 Ibid, p. 55.
47 Ibid, p. 55.
48 Ibid, pp. 47 & 50.
49 UNCN, *Report on Standing Committee 11, The Military Situation in and Relating to Namibia*, 1984, p. 3.
50 IDAF, *Apartheid's Army in Namibia: South Africa's Illegal Military Occupation*, 1982, p. 9.
51 Personal interview with author, Ovamboland, October 1985.
52 Reports on Human Rights abuses have been issued by, among others, Amnesty International, CCN, Namibia Communications Centre, IDAF, NSC, The South African Catholic Bishops' Conference, the British Council of Churches, and the British organisation Namibia Christian Exchange.
53 Personal interview with author, Ovamboland, October 1985.
54 Personal interview with author, Ovamboland, October 1985.
55 Personal interview with author, Ovamboland, October 1985.
56 *The Namibian*, 24.1.86.
57 Personal interview with author, Ovamboland, October 1985.
58 Personal interview with author, Ovamboland, October 1985.
59 Personal interview, Windhoek, October 1985.
60 *The Namibian*, 24.1.86.
61 Personal interview with author, Ovamboland, October 1985.
62 Personal interview with author, Windhoek, October 1985.

Chapter 3

1 FCO. United Kingdom Policy on Namibia, January 1986.
2 In 1983, France pulled out of the Contact Group in protest at the US policy of 'linkage'. France's voting pattern on the Security Council also appears to have changed since its withdrawal from the Contact Group.
3 *Hansard*, 4.12.74.
4 For fuller discussion of this theme, see Julio Faundez, "Is There Still a Role for International Law?", paper presented to the UNCN Regional Symposium on the International Effort to Implement Decree no. 1, Geneva 1984.
5 See Lord Trefgarne's speech in the House of Lords on the question of uranium imports from Namibia, *Hansard*, 23.4.1980.
6 Rio Tinto Zinc PLC owns 46.5% of Rössing Uranium Ltd's equity shares, but only 26.5% of the voting rights (CIIR, *Mines and Independence*, 1983, p. 37).
7 Rio Tinto Zinc Corporation PLC, Annual Report and Accounts, 1983, p. 7.
8 UN Centre on Transnational Corporations, Public Hearing on the Activities of TNCs in South Africa and Namibia, conference paper entitled, "TNCs with Interests in South Africa and Namibia", September 1985, pp. 34 − 36.
9 RTZ Corporation PLC, Annual Report and Accounts, 1984, p. 19.
10 Economist Intelligence Unit, Quarterly Economic Review, Annual Supplement on Namibia, 1985, p. 21.
11 UN Economic and Social Council, Commission on Transnational Corporations, Public Hearings on the activities of TNCs in South Africa and Namibia, Conference paper entitled, "Activities and Operations of TNCs in Namibia with Particular Emphasis on their Exploitation of Namibian Resources and their Contribution to and Support of South Africa's Illegal Occupation of Namibia", Report of Secretary General, September 1985, p. 19.
12 ODA Information Brief, September 1985.
13 Personal communication from ODA, November 1985.
14 Ibid., also ODA Information Brief, September 1985.
15 HMG Statistical Service, *British Aid Statistics 1979 − 1983*, 1984 edition.
16 Commonwealth Conference communiqués, October 1985.
17 *Hansard*, 4.12.74.
18 Letter from FCO to Oxfam 4.2.86.
19 Letter from Barclays Bank PLC to Oxfam 6.2.86.
20 Commonwealth Conference Communiqué, October 1985.
21 Text of address by His Excellency the President, Dr Kenneth David Kaunda, to the Joint Meeting of Foreign Ministers of the Frontline States and of the European Communities, held in Mulungushi Hall, Lusaka on Monday, 3rd February 1986.
22 ELOC commands wide support in Namibia. It is the largest single church in the country with some 400,000 members, nearly a third of the population. (Personal communication from the Namibia Communications Centre, November 1985.)
23 Extract from an article published in *Omakwetu*, ELOC's twice monthly magazine, October 1985, reproduced by the Namibia Communications Centre, 19.11.1985.
24 Personal interview with author, southern Namibia, Sept. 1985.

Summary and Key Considerations

1 Personal interview with author, southern Namibia, September 1985.

Appendices

APPENDIX I

Britain's voting record on Namibia at the UN Security Council

Date	No.	Description	UK Vote
1969 March	264	Recognises UN General Assembly's Resolution 2145 of 1966 describing South Africa's continued presence as illegal and calling for immediate withdrawal.	Abstained
August	269	Condemns South Africa's refusal to comply with SC Res.264 (above) by continuing to occupy Namibia; thus violating territorial integrity. Sets deadline for South Africa to withdraw by October 1969. Calls on all states to refrain from dealings with South Africa.	Abstained
1970 July	276	Asserts that South Africa's defiant attitude towards Security Council resolutions undermines UN's authority, calls on all member states especially those with economic and other interests in Namibia to refrain from any dealings with South Africa, decides to establish sub-committee to study ways of implementing SC resolutions.	Abstained
July	283	All UN member states to refrain from relations with South Africa over Namibia and cease investment activities including concessions in Namibia. United Nations Council for Namibia (UNCN) to make proposals regarding passports and visas for Namibians to travel abroad, and regarding the discouragement of tourism and emigration to Namibia. Recommends General Assembly to set up UN Fund for Namibia.	Abstained
July	284	Decides to submit to International Court of Justice question of legal consequences for UN member states of South Africa's continued presence in Namibia.	Abstained
1971 October	301	Condemns 'homelands' policy and South Africa's continued illegal presence, agrees with ICJ Advisory Opinion calling on all states to abstain from dealings with South Africa over Namibia, declares that foreign economic activities in Namibia are not subject to protection against claims of a future, lawful government of Namibia.	Abstained

1972	309	Requests UN Secretary General to initiate contacts with all concerned to effectNamibia's independence.	For
February	310	Condemns South Africa's refusal to comply with UN over Namibia, calls upon South African Government to abolish any labour system within Namibia which contravenes Universal Declaration of Human Rights, and calls upon all member States to ensure these basic provisions are adhered to by foreign companies, considers that South Africa's continued occupation of Namibia is detrimental to maintenance of peace and security in the region and that South Africa should withdraw immediately, and that SC should meet to decide effective measures under UN Charter to secure implementation of this resolution.	Abstained
August	319	Invites the Secretary General to continue contacts with all concerned to effect Namibia's independence.	For
December	323	Notes that majority of Namibians consulted by UN are opposed to 'homelands' policy, and in favour of South Africa's withdrawal.	For
1973 December	342	Notes Secretary General's report, and decides to discontinue further efforts on the basis of SC Res. 309.	For
1974 December	366	Calls on South Africa to withdraw from Namibia, set deadline of 30 May 1975 for withdrawal, and calls for transfer of power to the people of Namibia with the assistance of the UN.	For
1975 June	SC draft resolution No. S/11713	Determining that the illegal occupation of Namibia by South Africa constitutes a threat to international peace and security, demanding that South Africa proceed with necessary steps to withdraw from Namibia. Draft resolution fails due to UK, US and French veto.	Veto
1976 January	385	Demands South Africa withdraw and transfer power to the people of Namibia, calls for the holding of 'free and fair' elections under UN supervision and control.	For
October	SC draft resolution No. S/12211	Determines that the illegal occupation of Namibia and the war there constitutes a threat to international peace and security under Chapter VII of the UN Charter, and that all states should prevent any form of military collaboration with South Africa including sales of military equipment. Draft resolution fails due to UK, US and French veto.	Veto
1978 May	428 (On Angola)	Condemns South Africa's aggression against Angola, demands immediate withdrawal of all South African forces from Angola, demands South Africa end its illegal occupation of Namibia.	For
July	431	UN Secretary General to appoint Special Representative for Namibia to submit report with recommendations for implementation of SC Res. 385 for free and fair elections under UN supervision.	For
July	432	Notes that Walvis Bay is an integral part of Namibia, and South Africa must not use it in any manner prejudicial to the independence of Namibia, or to Namibia's economy.	For
September	435	Calls for free and fair elections for the whole of Namibia as one political entity under the control and	For

supervision of the UN; universal adult suffrage; after national elections, a national Constitution for an independent Namibia; before start of electoral campaign, Namibia's Administrator-General to repeal all remaining discriminatory or restrictive laws, regulations and administrative measures. Before start of electoral campaign, South Africa to release all Namibian political prisoners and detainees; all Namibian refugees to be allowed to return peacefully and participate fully in electoral process, the UN to ensure that Namibians in exile are given free and voluntary choice to return; a binding ceasefire by all partners and the restriction of South Africa and SWAPO armed forces to base, thereafter a phased withdrawal from Namibia of the majority of South African troops; all unilateral measures taken by the South African Government in Namibia in relation to the electoral process null and void.

December	439	Condemns South Africa's decision to proceed unilaterally with the internal 'elections' for the Democratic Turnhalle Alliance, and demands that South Africa cooperate with Security Council in implementation of SC Res. 435.	Abstained
1979 March	447	Calls for South Africa to cease armed invasion of Angola, and calls for member states to extend P assistance to Angola.	Abstained
November	454 (On Angola)	Calls upon South Africa to cease all acts of aggression against Angola, demands that South Africa desist from using Namibia to launch acts of aggression against Angola or other neighbouring states.	Abstained
1980 June	475	Demands South Africa withdraw armed forces from Angola, calls on all states to impose arms embargo against South Africa, calls for payment of compensation to Angola by South Africa for damage to life and property resulting from acts of military aggression.	Abstained
1981 April	SC draft resolution No. S/14459	Condemns South Africa for its continued illegal occupation of Namibia, decides to adopt effective measures including economic and political sanctions, oil and arms embargoes against South Africa. Draft resolution fails due to UK, US, and French veto.	Veto
April	Revised SC draft resolution No. S/14460 Rev.1	Reiterates that Namibia is the legal responsibility of the UN until self-determination is achieved, and that all member states should sever diplomatic, consular and trade relations with South Africa. Draft resolution fails due to UK, US and French veto.	Veto
April	SC draft resolution No. S/14461	Decides to impose a mandatory embargo on the direct and indirect supply of products to South Africa and occupied Namibia. Draft resolution fails due to US, UK and French veto.	Veto
April	SC draft resolution No. S/14462	Decides that all member states shall cease any provision to South Africa of arms and related materials of all types. Draft resolution fails due to UK, US and French veto.	Veto

August	Revised SC draft resolution No. S/14664 Rev.2 (On Angola)	Demands immediate withdrawal of all South African troops from Angola, urges all member states to extend material assistance to Angola, decides to send a Commission of Investigation to Angola. Draft resolution fails due to US veto.	Abstained
1983 May	532	UN Secretary General mandated to consult all parties concerned on a timetable for implementation of Res. 435, and on proposed ceasefire. Secretary General to report to Security Council by 31st August 1983.	For
October	539	Extends UN Secretary General's mandate (see Res. 532 above) to 31 December 1983; condemns South Africa for obstructing implementation of SC Res. 435; reiterates SC Res. 435; and rejects South Africa linking independence of Namibia to irrelevant and extraneous issues incompatible with SC Res. 435 (referring to the United States' 'linkage' policy. The US abstained in the voting).	For
December	545 (On Angola)	Condemns South Africa's continued military occupation of parts of southern Angola, demands that South Africa should withdraw all its forces, and considers that Angola is entitled to redress for material damage suffered.	For
1984 January	546 (On Angola)	Condemns renewed South African military aggression in Angola, condemns South Africa for using Namibian territory as a springboard for perpetuating armed attacks and for sustaining its occupation of parts of Angola. Demands South Africa cease all bombing and acts of aggression in Angola, and the withdrawal of all South African military forces from Angola. Calls for all member states to implement arms embargo imposed against South Africa in SC Res. 418 of 1977, calls for compensation to Angola.	Abstained
December	558	Reaffirms SC Res. 418 of 1977 (deciding on mandatory arms embargo against South Africa) and SC Res. 421 (committee established to make arms embargo against South Africa more effective), requests member states to refrain from exporting arms, ammunition, and military vehicles to South Africa.	For
1985 June	566	Condemns South Africa's continued illegal occupation of Namibia in defiance of UN; condemns South Africa for installing interim Multi Party Conference (MPC) government in Namibia, declares installation of MPC to be null and void, declares that no UN member state shall recognise it, and demands that South Africa rescind; warns South Africa that continued failure to cooperate on implementation of SC Res. 435 would compel Security Council to consider adoption of sanctions; urges UN member states to undertake specified economic sanctions.	Abstained
July	569 (On South Africa)	Strongly condemns establishment of 'State of Emergency' in various districts of South Africa, as well as the mass arrests, detention and murders in South Africa; calls for unconditional release of all political prisoners in South Africa; urges UN member	Abstained

		states to suspend all new investments, prohibit the sale of krugerrands, restrict sporting and cultural relations, suspend guaranteed export loans, prohibit new contracts in the nuclear field, and prohibit all sales of computer equipment which may be used by the South African army and police.	
November	**SC draft resolution** S/17633	Proposed a decision to impose mandatory selective sanctions against South Africa under Chapter VII of the UN Charter (see section on International Law) listing: oil embargo, arms embargo, prohibition of all new investments in South Africa and Namibia, prohibition of all new government bank loans and credit guarantees to South African Government and MPC interim government in Namibia, termination of all export credit guarantees for exports to South Africa and Namibia, prohibition of importation or enrichment of uranium from Namibia and South Africa, prohibition of supply of technology, equipment and licences for nuclear plants in South Africa, prohibition of visits to and from South Africa and Namibia by military, security, intelligence, and other defence personnel, prohibition of sale and export of computers capable of being used by South African army, police, and security forces, cessation of funding for trade missions, termination of double taxation agreements with South Africa, prohibition of krugerrand sales. Draft resolution fails due to US and UK veto.	**Veto**

NB. Except where indicated otherwise, all the above SC Resolutions are on Namibia only.

APPENDIX 2

UNITED NATIONS

NAMIBIA GAZETTE No.1

DECREE No. 1
FOR THE PROTECTION OF THE NATURAL RESOURCES OF NAMIBIA

Conscious of its responsibility to protect the natural resources of the people of Namibia and of ensuring that these natural resources are not exploited to the detriment of Namibia, its people or environmental assets, the United Nations Council for Namibia enacts the following decree:

DECREE

The United Nations Council for Namibia,

Recognizing that, in the terms of General Assembly resolution 2145 (XXI) of 27 October 1966 the Territory of Namibia (formerly South West Africa) is the direct responsibility of the United Nations,

Accepting that this responsibility includes the obligation to support the right of the people of Namibia to achieve self-government and independence in accordance with General Assembly resolution 1514 (XV) of 14 December 1960,

Reaffirming that the Government of the Republic of South Africa is in illegal possession of the Territory of Namibia,

Furthering the decision of the General Assembly in resolution 1803 (XVII) of 14 December 1962 which declared the right of peoples and nations to permanent sovereignty over their natural wealth and resources,

Noting that the Government of the Republic of South Africa has usurped and interfered with these rights,

Desirous of securing for the people of Namibia adequate protection of the natural wealth and resources of the Territory which is rightfully theirs,

Recalling the advisory opinion of the International Court of Justice of 21 June 1971,[1]

Acting in terms of the powers conferred on it by General Assembly resolution 2248 (S-V) of 19 May 1967 and all other relevant resolutions and decisions regarding Namibia,

---

[1]*Legal Consequences for States of the Continued Presence of South Africa in Namibia (South West Africa) notwithstanding Security Council Resolution 276 (1970), Advisory Opinion, I.C.J. Reports 1971,* p. 16.

Decrees that

1. No person or entity, whether a body corporate or unincorporated, may search for, prospect for, explore for, take, extract, mine, process, refine, use, sell, export, or distribute any natural resource, whether animal or mineral, situated or found to be situated within the territorial limits of Namibia without the consent and permission of the United Nations Council for Namibia or any person authorized to act on its behalf for the purpose of giving such permission or such consent;

2. Any permission, concession or licence for all or any of the purposes specified in paragraph 1 above whensoever granted by any person or entity, including any body purporting to act under the authority of the Government of the Republic of South Africa or the "Administration of South West Africa" or their predecessors, is null, void and of no force or effect;

3. No animal resource, mineral, or other natural resource produced in or emanating from the Territory of Namibia may be taken from the said Territory by any means whatsoever to any place whatsoever outside the territorial limits of Namibia by any person or body, whether corporate or unincorporated, without the consent and permission of the United Nations Council for Namibia or of any person authorized to act on behalf of the said Council;

4. Any animal, mineral or other natural resource produced in or emanating from the Territory of Namibia which shall be taken from the said Territory without the consent and written authority of the United Nations Council for Namibia or of any person authorized to act on behalf of the said Council may be seized and shall be forfeited to the benefit of the said Council and held in trust by them for the benefit of the people of Namibia;

5. Any vehicle, ship or container found to be carrying animal, mineral or other natural resources produced in or emanating from the Territory of Namibia shall also be subject to seizure and forfeiture by or on behalf of the United Nations Council for Namibia or of any person authorized to act on behalf of the said Council and shall be forfeited to the benefit of the said Council and held in trust by them for the benefit of the people of Namibia;

6. Any person, entity or corporation which contravenes the present decree in respect of Namibia may be held liable in damages by the future Government of an independent Namibia;

7. For the purposes of the preceding paragraphs 1, 2, 3, 4 and 5 and in order to give effect to this decree, the United Nations Council for Namibia hereby authorizes the United Nations Commissioner for Namibia, in accordance with resolution 2248 (S-V), to take the necessary steps after consultations with the President.

The foregoing is the text of the Decree adopted by the United Nations Council for Namibia at its 209th meeting on 27 September 1974 and approved by the General Assembly of the United Nations at its 29th Session on 13 December 1974. For additional copies and information, please communicate with the United Nations Commissioner for Namibia, Room DC-328, United Nations, New York, N.Y. 10017 or at the Office of the United Nations Commissioner for Namibia, Box 33550, Lusaka, Zambia.

APPENDIX 3

Transnational corporations based in the UK and Northern Ireland with interests in companies in Namibia

600 GROUP LTD.
ACROW LTD.
AE PLC
BABCOCK INTERNATIONAL PLC
BARCLAYS BANK PLC
B.A.T. INDUSTRIES GROUP
BEECHAM GROUP PLC
BERGER, JENSON & NICHOLSON
BESTOBELL PLC
BICC LTD.
BLACKWOOD HODGE PLC[1]
BLUE CIRCLE INDUSTRIES PLC
BL PLC
THE BOC GROUP PLC
BRITISH PETROLEUM CO. PLC[2]
THE BRITISH PETROLEUM COMPANY LTD.[3]
BRITISH PRINTING & COMMUNICATION CORPORATION PLC
BRITISH STEEL CORPORATION[2]
BUSH BOAKE ALLEN
CHARTER CONSOLIDATED PLC
COMMERCIAL UNION ASSURANCE CO. PLC
CONSOLIDATED GOLD FIELDS PLC
C.T. BOWRING & CO. LTD.[4]
DELTA GROUP PLC
THE DISTILLERS CO. PLC
GENERAL ELECTRIC COMPANY PLC
GRAND METROPOLITAN PLC
GUARDIAN ROYAL EXCHANGE ASSURANCE PLC
JOHN DAVIS & SON (DERBY) LTD.
LONRHO LTD.
MINET HOLDINGS LTD.
MITCHELL COTTS GROUP PLC
NORTHERN ENGINEERING INDUSTRIES PLC
NORWICH UNION & GENERAL ASSURANCE
RIO TINTO ZINC CORPORATION PLC
ROYAL DOULTON TABLEWARE (HOLDINGS)
ROYAL INSURANCE PLC
STC INTERNATIONAL COMPUTERS LTD. PLC
SEDGWICK GROUP PLC
THE SHELL TRANSPORT & TRADING CO.[5]
SMITH INDUSTRIES LTD.
STANDARD CHARTERED BANK PLC
SUN ALLIANCE & LONDON INSURANCE
WITTINGDON INVESTMENTS LTD.
YARROW & CO. LTD.

Footnotes

1   Wholly owned by Blackwood Hodge South Africa Ltd. which in turn is wholly owned by the British parent.
2   Controlled by the UK Government.
3   The British Petroleum Co. Ltd. is the parent of Standard Oil Co. (Sohio), United States of America, through British Petroleum (Overseas) BV, Netherlands.
4   A subsidiary of Marsh and McLennan Companies, Inc., United States of America.
5   The Royal Dutch Petroleum Company, Netherlands, together with The Shell Transport and Trading Company, United Kingdom, form the Royal Dutch/Shell group of companies. The Shell Transport and Trading Company owns 40% of the equity and the Royal Dutch Petroleum Company owns the remaining 60% of the equity in the Royal Dutch/Shell group. These two companies own these proportions of the equity in all of the subsidiaries and affiliates of the group, including its Namibian operations. The subsidiaries are held through the holding companies, The Shell Petroleum Co. Ltd., United Kingdom, and Shell Petroleum NV, Netherlands.

Source: UN Centre on Transnational Corporations, Public Hearings on the Activities of Transnational Corporations in South Africa, and Namibia, conference paper 'TNCs with Interests in South Africa and Namibia', September 1985, pp. 34 — 36.

Abbreviations

AG	Administrator-General
CCN	Namibia Council of Churches
CDM	Consolidated Diamond Mines
CIIR	Catholic Institute for International Relations
DTA	Democratic Turnhalle Alliance
EEC	European Economic Community
EEZ	Exclusive Economic Zone
ELOC	The Evangelical Lutheran Ovambo Kavango Church of Namibia
FCO	Foreign & Commonwealth Office
GDP	Gross Domestic Product
GENCOR	General Mining Union Corporation Ltd.
GNP	Gross National Product
ICI	Imperial Chemical Industries PLC
ICJ	International Court of Justice
ICSEAF	International Commission for the Southeast Atlantic Fisheries
IDAF	International Defence and Aid Fund
IMF	International Monetary Fund
IMR	Infant Mortality Rate (0-1 years)
MPC	Multi-Party Conference
MPLA	Popular Liberation Movement of Angola
MRG	Minority Rights Group
NLP	Namibia Literacy Programme
NSC	Namibia Support Committee
OAU	Organisation of African Unity
ODA	Overseas Development Administration
PHC	Primary Health Care
R	Rand
RTZ	Rio Tinto Zinc Corporation PLC
SA	South Africa
SACC	South African Council of Churches
SADF	South African Defence Force
SWA	South West Africa
SWANLA	South West Africa Native Labour Association
SWAPO	South West Africa People's Organisation
SWATF	South West African Territorial Force
TCL	Tsumeb Corporation Ltd.
TNC	Transnational Corporation
UN	United Nations
UNCN	United Nations Council for Namibia
UNETPSA	United Nations Educational Training Programme for Southern Africa
UNGA	United Nations General Assembly
UNIN	United Nations Institute for Namibia
UNSC	United Nations Security Council

Bibliography

- **A Future for Namibia series, Catholic Institute for International Relations, London.**
  1. *Namibia in the 1980s*, CIIR/British Council of Churches, 1981.
  2. Richard Moorsom, *Agriculture: Transforming a Wasted Land*, 1982.
  3. *Mining: Mines and Independence*, 1983.
  4. Justin Ellis, *Education, Repression and Liberation*, CIIR/World University Service, 1984.
  5. Richard Moorsom, *Fishing and Exploiting the Sea*, 1984.
  6. J. Hanlon, *Beggar your Neighbour, Apartheid Power in Southern Africa*, CIIR and James Currey, 1986 (forthcoming).
- **United Nations Publications**
  Trust Betrayed: Namibia, 1974.
  Namibia: a Unique UN Responsibility, 1983
  Social Conditions in Namibia: Report of the UN Council for Namibia, 1983 .
  Contacts between UN Member States and South Africa: Report of Standing Committee II of the UN Council for Namibia, 1984.
  Plunder of Namibian Uranium: Major Findings of the Hearings on Namibian Uranium held by the Council for Namibia in July 1980, 1982. UN Council for Namibia, *Annual Reports*
- **International Defence and Aid Fund Publications**
  Namibia: the facts, 1980.
  Fact papers:
  9. *Remember Kassinga*, 1981.
  10. *Apartheid's Army in Namibia*, 1982.
  13. *A Nation in Peril: Health in Apartheid Namibia*, 1985.
  Focus, bimonthly news digest of political repression in Namibia and South Africa
- **Other Publications**
  Alun Roberts, *The Rössing File: The Inside Story of Britain's Secret Contract for Namibian Uranium*, Namibia Support Committee, The Campaign against the Namibian Uranium Contract (CANUC), London, 1980.
  Tim Lobstein/NSC Health Collective (eds), *Namibia: Reclaiming the People's Health*, Action on Namibia Publications, London, 1984.
  Department of Information and Publicity SWAPO, *To Be Born a Nation: The Liberation Struggle for Namibia*, Zed Press, London, 1981.
  Tore Linne Eriksen with Richard Moorsom, *The Political Economy of Namibia: An Annotated Critical Bibliography*, Scandinavian Institute of African Studies, Uppsala, 1985.
  R.H. Green, K. Kiljunen & M-L Kiljunen (eds), *Namibia: the Last Colony*, Longman, Harlow, 1981.